BY RAIL THROUGH THE HEART OF

By Rail Through the Heart of Ireland

by

Padraic O'Farrell

THE MERCIER PRESS

THE MERCIER PRESS LIMITED
4 Bridge Street, Cork.
24 Lower Abbey Street, Dublin 1.

© P. O'Farrell, 1990

British Library Cataloguing in Publication Data
O'Farrell, Padraic
    By rail through the heart of Ireland
    1. Ireland. Description & travel.
    I. Title.
    914 . 1504824

ISBN 0 - 85342 - 948 - 0

To Carmel, Maeve and Peg

Printed in the Republic of Ireland by
Litho Press, Main Street, Midleton, Co. Cork.

Contents

Foreword	vii
Acknowledgements	ix
1. Background	9
2. Setting out: Dublin and Co. Kildare	15
3. Co. Laois	38
4. Co. Tipperary	47
5. Co. Limerick and Co. Cork	63
6. Destination	81
References	87

Foreword

A few words of advice to the traveller on the Dublin-Cork line who wishes to use this book as a companion. A number of the old railway stations mentioned are no longer in use; others are levelled, signal boxes and other trappings removed. Landmarks, especially notable ones, are alluded to. You will need to be alert in order to spot them while passing. Therefore I suggest that you:
(a) read this book before travelling and note places of particular interest which merit a close lookout.
(b) browse through it *en route*, but hop across long passages and keep up with the journey's progress.

Better still, enjoy a comfortable, relaxed train trip and read this celebration of the countryside, checking briefly on towns and more prominent landmarks.

Go neirí an bóthar iarann leat!

Padraic O'Farrell

Acknowledgements

I wish to acknowledge permission to use copyright material and other valuable assistance so generously given by the following: Cyril Ferris and Mary Linehan, Media and Publications Department, Iarnród Éireann; Bord Fáilte (Rosaleen Clarke); Irish Railway Record Society (K. A. Murray); Library Officers Hanna O'Sullivan and Kieran Burke (Cork), Cáit Kavanagh (Laois), Anne Coughlan (Offaly), Michael Kavanagh (Kildare), Tom Deegan (Tipperary); Desmond Egan; Michael O'Brien; Con Costello; E. Dillon & Co. (Maureen Sullivan); Oriel Press, Charleville (Ted O'Riordan); Irish Racing Board (Tom Burke, Limerick Junction); Bórd na Móna (John Crowe); Electricity Supply Board (Ronnie Persse); Royal Dublin Society (David Grey and Alice Purdon); *The Irish Times; The Cork Examiner* (Vincent Kelly); The National Museum of Ireland.

Padraic O'Farrell

CHAPTER ONE

BACKGROUND

The prophecies of St Colmcille were thought to have had the arrival of the steam-train in mind when they proclaimed:

> In both north and south iron wheels shall support, fiery chariots, which shall resemble druidical deception.

Railways did in fact arrive in 1834 when experimental runs took place on the newly laid Dublin-Kingstown line and record speeds were reached.

In September 1841, Tory leader Sir Robert Peel received from a group of Dublin businessmen, a proposal to establish a single railway system for all Ireland. They had seen the success of the Dublin-Kingstown line and the Ulster Railway. Their new company was to be called the Great Southern and Western Railway (GS & WR) and the first stage of its line to Cork was to run from Dublin to Cashel, Co. Tipperary. Despite some opposition from the Grand Canal Company, the bill for its incorporation became law on 6 August 1844. Although the Cashel terminus was eventually abandoned to allow a direction west of the Galtee mountains, the share stocks of the company were known as 'Cashels' throughout the existence of the GS & WR.

Headquarters was to be at Kingsbridge but this was quite a distance from the city centre. Opponents of the idea pointed to the traffic congestion at Watling St Bridge, caused by an archway known as Richmond Tower. Flamboyantly, the company had this removed to the entrance of the Royal Hospital.

Major General Pasley, a British army engineer, was given the task of deciding on a suitable gauge. He received the opinions of a number of experts before deciding on

5'3". An unauthenticated story alleged that he took the 6'2" gauge of the Ulster line (considered too broad) and the standard gauge (4' 8½"), rounded both off to 6' and 4'6" respectively, split the difference and came up with 5'3" — a simple way of dealing with the Irish Problem, rail-wise!

Branch lines were envisaged and a track to Carlow from Cherryville, Co. Kildare, was included in the first stage. The renowned railway contractor William Dargan, along with William McCormack, secured the initial contracts. McCormack was to complete a line to Hazlehatch. Dargan was to bring it as far as Sallins. The two were to join forces then in laying the branch to Carlow before continuing with the main line.

The first sod was cut in January 1845 at Adamstown, near Lucan. The Duke of Leinster performed the ceremony and a cynical onlooker, a labouring man, shouted that he could die happy after 'seeing a duke working like any common man'. Spectacular progress ensured an August 1846 opening to traffic. The main line to Portlaoise was operating in June 1847 and trains reached Thurles in March 1848. These were famine times in Ireland and consequently a luxury like a railway line, despite the employment it gave, had its begrudgers. Intimidation of workers was commonplace; overseers were attacked and at least three were murdered.

Despite steady progress, the people of Cork were getting impatient. They did not like the idea of a branch line being laid before the main one was completed. They threatened to form their own company, so the GS & WR finished their piecemeal contracting and paid Dargan £600,000 to complete the seventy-eight remaining miles from Thurles to Cork.

Meanwhile, the Waterford and Limerick line (W & LR) was laid as far as Limerick Junction so when the GS & WR reached there, Dublin was connected with Limerick. Cork people were again annoyed at the upstaging.

Difficult terrain faced the builders and embankments, bridges and a viaduct over the Blackwater river had to be constructed. Blasting operations were common as the rocky hills guarding the valley of the River Martin were penetrated. Thousands of men were employed in this final assault and on 18 October 1849, a train bearing the directors of the GS & WR averaged thirty miles per hour and arrived at a temporary terminus at Blackpool. The tunnelling beneath Cork city to a quayside station took place later. Its 1,238.5 metres took until 3 December 1855 to complete. Cashel, first mooted as an intermediate station, was forgotten about until 1904 when a branch line linked it with Goold's Cross.

Thus the 'premier line' went into business with 'down' and 'up' day mails taking seven hours, and others, carrying third-class passengers, taking a marathon twelve hours as they stopped at every station. Initially a night mail ran only to Mallow but its run was soon extended to Cork. A complex shunting system at Limerick Junction caused big delays so the best time from Dublin to Cork was about four and a half hours. A railway hotel was established here to refresh tired passengers (Dublin and Cork also had company hotels). Yet the GS & WR had comfortable furnishings, not at all like what was experienced on some British lines. An early pamphlet had this to say about mail trains and 'third-class waggons':

> Nothing but direct necessity will compel a man, however poor he may be, to travel by these legalized nuisances, and that if he have any regard to either health or comfort, he is obliged however ill he can afford it, to go by a second-class open carriage, which is not very comfortable either.

A satirical comment on the behaviour of a certain class of passenger was given by a Dublin contributor to an early publication entitled *Tales of the Rail*:

> Should you be gifted with a voice suggestive of the melody of a consumptive fog-horn, or a falsetto articulation, always give your vocal chords full scope,

and relieve the ample reservoir of your loquacity by retailing all the inane gossip and petty scandals at your command. In regard to the topics most calculated to delight your fellow travellers, that, of course, entirely rests with yourself — the platform is yours. That you are acquainted with certain members of the Royal family goes without saying; at the same time you should not be oblivious to the fact that a judicious and familiar reference to 'Lord Charlie', 'Sir George' and 'dear Lady Gertrude' will instil into the minds of your listeners a sense of your exalted social position and intimate acquaintance with the aristocracy. Should you have a relative in the army who has risen to the dazzling rank of corporal, always refer to him as 'The Colonel'. The guards of this line, being particularly caring and obliging, will afford you a choice opportunity of asserting your importance.

An illuminating example of their caring nature can be seen by a notice placed on a third-class carriage of the Dublin-Cork train in the late nineteenth century. It read:

> If the gentleman who left a baby in the 3rd class rly carriage on 25th ult. does not claim the same within a fortnight, it will be sold to defray expenses.

But let us get back on the rails!

In 1922 an 'American Mail' brought transatlantic post from Cobh along a suburban line to Cork, up to Dublin and Kingstown (Dun Laoghaire) from where it crossed the channel to Holyhead. Many transatlantic passengers preferred to use this to get to London too, because it saved them more hours on the liner.

During the War of Independence and the Civil War, there were assorted derailings, hold-ups and blowing up of bridges along the route. Tipperary, Limerick and Cork were to the fore in both of these struggles, so that by the end of 1922 only two-thirds of GS & WR lines were actually carrying trains. A Railway Defence and Maintenance Corps was formed by the new Free State authorities, to patrol the railway lines and repair damage. The government also called for greater amalgamation of the system in order to bring more coherence into it. Therefore, by the end of 1925 the Great Southern Railway embraced a number of former rivals.

Parcel delivery, race and horse-show specials, excursions and other innovations were introduced by degrees, while the company developed its engineering works and built its own engines and rolling-stock. 'Standardisation' was introduced and a 1932 booklet elaborated on charges for zebras, pumas, hyenas, bears, wolves, jackals, tiger cats, deer, monkeys, elephants, lions, sea lions, camels and ostriches. Oblivious to the passengers, these were transported at the owners risk! Other merchandise included bees (live), feather boas, corpses, ashes of cremated bodies, ships' compasses, wreaths (artificial), busts (ladies), machines (bacon slicing, bone grinding), periscopes, magic lanterns, stuffed birds, animals and fishes, foster mothers (chicken rearers), wine in jars or bottles, X-ray tubes, rocking horses, meggers, stags' heads, feathers, aeroplane wings, corset stands, limbs (artificial), magic lanterns, and many more.

During the Second World War many passengers who had left the railways for their private motor-cars, returned. They were punished for their sin of desertion by long delays due to part-substitution of turf for coal in the fireboxes of the steam-engines. As a result, many branch lines were then closed.

With the amalgamation of the GSR and the Dublin United Transport Company on 1 January 1945, Córas Iompair Éireann (CIE) became the main authority for the provision of public transport in Ireland. A wheel logo was emblazoned on coaches, and quick-witted Dubliners named it the 'Flying Snail'. The Grand Canal Company and CIE were amalgamated in 1950 when the 1950 Traffic Act set up a new Board. In the same year, CIE was nationalised. The Board was reconstituted in 1958. In 1960 the railway hotels came under a new company, Ostlanna Iompair Éireann Teoranta.

Improvements continued in passenger and goods services. Tracks were upgraded, new speeds were attained, extra journeys were put into operation and container traffic was introduced. After the war, petrol had become freely available once again and road transport began to be used more for freight while passengers again forsook the railways. For economy, Drum battery-trains were experimented with, and a turf burning locomotive underwent trials on the Dublin-Cork line. As the steam age drew to an end, diesel engines were introduced and new coaches were manufactured at the company's Inchicore works. The days were numbered for the pride of the 'premier line', the powerful three cylinder 4-6-0s built at Inchicore in 1939 whose names were selected from Ireland's rich store of legend — *Maedbh, Macha* and *Tailte*. The mid-sixties saw the final abolition of steam for all but nostalgic trips undertaken by keen railway enthusiasts.

The sixties also witnessed the arrival of stewardesses on the Dublin-Cork line (1959 to 1975). Livery and services improved and special excursion fares attracted customers who realised that petrol and parking costs made driving expensive. Further improvements were introduced in 1987 when on 2 February the Transport (Reorganisation of CIE) Act of 1986 came into effect. It gave separate identities to the transport systems operating within the company. The inter-city service upon which we are about to travel joined with the new electrified DART under the banner of Iarnród Éireann, Irish Rail. With the outline of the noble history that lies behind their fresh logo, let us board the Dublin-Cork Inter-City Express. And as it whisks us through the midlands and beyond to the city on the Lee, let us enjoy a little of the history, the tales and even a few lies associated with the countryside through which we speed.

CHAPTER TWO

SETTING OUT: DUBLIN AND CO. KILDARE

A definite article can make a world of difference in Dublin. Kingsbridge is the old name for its chief railway station but 'The Kingsbridge' is the Liffey crossing from Parkgate Street. Linger on its centre and read the bronze plaque which tells that in 1955 Cumann na h-Úaigeanna Náisiúnta (The National Graves Association) renamed it Seán Heuston Bridge, after a young patriot of the 1916 rebellion who was a clerk in the Great Southern and Western Railway Company. From the Mendicity Institute at Usher's Island just two bridges downstream he, accompanied by a few comrades, held down a large force of British troops in the Royal Barracks.

Admire the four lamps on the parapet and, in case we forget to look back when we move to catch our train, lean over and see the date (1821) in ornate metal, on the river side.

A still, crisp, frosty morning, a weak sun washing the silhouette of old Dublin, smoke from the stacks of Guinness' Brewery easing down to encircle its 150 foot tall 'onion tower'; the mordant smell of malting recalls the reverence in which its product was held by a rhymester in M.J. McManus' *Dublin Diversions:*

> The Brewery at St James' Gate
> Has made the name of Guinness great
> The publican who passes that
> Must genuflect and raise his hat

Opposite, the gentle rise to the soul and the sin of Dublin. The Cathedral of the Holy Trinity, better known as Christ Church, stands on a site chosen by King Sitric in 1038 for a wooden chapel. It still manages to thrust a dignified spire and part of its transept above and about the capped rubic-cube-style civic offices. Down around there was Smock Alley Theatre and Fishamble Street 'Musick Hall' where Handel first performed his *Messiah* in public.

St Patrick's Cathedral stands aloof, regally exposed in glorious condemnation of the wrong perpetrated against its neighbour. Because Celtic chapels were not dedicated to canonised saints except in the case of a founder, it is claimed that the original St Patrick's was established by the patron himself. Jonathan Swift was appointed its dean in 1713 and is buried there. Part of W.B. Yeats' translation of 'The Dane's' self-composed epitaph is pertinent:

> Swift has sailed into his rest;
> Savage indignation there
> Cannot lacerate his breast.
> Imitate him, if you dare,
> World-besotted traveller; he
> Served human liberty.

This is the area of the Liberties, once peopled by weavers and tailors, the site of 'Old' St Audeon's church and the last remaining city gate, with the river Poddle below, completing a self-spun tapestry of old Dublin town. Just close your eyes and recall small company trains trundling along narrow street tracks. Remember, too, the bustle of barges being loaded at Victoria Quay nearby and their proud snouts parting the Liffey waters as they head for the Port of Dublin below, funnels lowered when passing under a bridge at high tide. Oh, and don't forget the gurrier on the grime-grey wall hailing the proud skipper and jibing 'Hey mister! Bring us back a parrot!'

With the senses primed, open your eyes and study the downstream *mise-en-scène*. On the near left is the Esplanade of Collins Barracks, the aforementioned Royal Barracks. This is the oldest occupied military post in the world, named after a Corkman who brought a mighty nation to the treaty table in 1921 and thereby signed his

Heuston Station Dublin (formerly Kingsbridge)

own death warrant. Further down, the building that triggered off the Civil War which brought about his death — the Four Courts. Its magnificent Gandon dome is a shapely green eminence in the grey morning. At one time an underground tunnel passed under the river from its precincts and emerged at Christ Church. It was used in later years for storing church furnishings. Once an army officer attending a funeral there wandered through the tunnel and was locked inside. Much later, it was opened and his skeleton was discovered still grasping his sword and the remains of over 200 rats strewn around — those that perished before vast numbers overpowered him.

But there is a train to catch and much more to see, so let us leave the bridge and admire the fine granite headquarters of Córas Iompair Éireann, the Irish Transport Authority. It resembles a great Renaissance house, with its Corinthian pillars, festoons, rustications, ornamentations and balustrade. CIE has had its share of industrial disputes and it is amusing to recall that the 1848 completion of this building was four years behind schedule – owing to a masons' strike!

A Bath architect, Sancton Wood, built it for the Great Southern and Western Railway. The reception desk in its entrance hall bears the crests of that company, the Dublin and South East Railway, the Great Northern Railway Board, the Great Southern Railway, Dublin United Tramway Company (1896) Ltd and the Midland and Great Western Railway of Ireland (1845). The entrance to the train platforms is around the corner in St John's Road. Victorian, it has eight columns and four attractive lights. Some brass window-ledges have been well shone by the bags of thousands of travellers.

Across the street is the 1900 Dispensary of Dr Steevens' Hospital and its Queen Anne-shaped Nurses' Home, belying its Victorian origin. Grissel Steevens built the hospital from her father's legacy. She herself occupied an apartment in the building. An old story tells how a certain bad-tempered Dublin lady refused alms to a beggarwoman who arrived at her door, surrounded by children, one day.

'Be off with you and your litter of piglets,' she screamed.

The offended pauper placed a curse on the lady, and in later life she gave birth to an infant with a pig's snout. The baby was Grissel. Typical of untrue gossip, the tale survived despite the fact that Grissel Steevens was quite a handsome woman.

The traveller who arrives too early might drop up to the Royal Hospital, Kilmainham, now splendidly renovated and hosting assorted exhibitions and functions. The fine plaster and wood carvings of its church and dining-hall are particularly attractive. It is easy to imagine its 'Chelsea Pensioners' strolling about the grounds. Even from where we stand, the clock tower of its elegant seventeenth-century William Robinson design can be seen to the right.

Within the station and past the ticket-office, the bustle of a busy main terminus reverberates around two and a half acres of trainshed, supported by seventy-two iron pillars. Black and white squares of terrazzo are suddenly

Iarnród Éireann Inter-City train

familiar, because arrivals and departures of Cork and Kerry hurlers, footballers and supporters at All-Ireland Final time are a feature of Irish photographic journalism.

The 'Railwayman's Bar', a restaurant and a bookshop face the large timetable. The next Cork train will depart from Platform 2 at 12.45 hours and will leave on time; it informs:

> 'Change at Limerick Junction for Limerick.'
> 'Change at Mallow for Banteer, Millstreet,
> Farrenfore and Tralee.'

'Super'– and 'Standard'– class refreshment cars are promised.

Already the orange and black, sleek Inter-City engine is snorting its eagerness to be under way. There is still time, however, to study the destinations of trains leaving from the four main platforms and to go looking for Platform 1, outside the sheltered area.

On the way there, a bronze plate demands a close perusal. It bears the names of ninety-seven members of the GS & WR 'who laid down their lives for their country in the Great War 1914-1918'. This is significant, because Platform 1 is still known to older CIE employees as the 'military siding'. It was used for troop movement to and from the Curragh and provincial garrisons. But the Irish soldiers of the Crown were not allowed mix with the gentle passengers on the other platforms, even on their way to death on the Western Front. Rail transportation of formations was always considerable; as early as 1869 a *Handbook of Railway Distances* was published by Walter Westcott Bronway for the Secretary of State for War and was revised by the Railway Clearing House, Dublin. A detailed document, it made planning easy. For example, a lift from Parsonstown, King's County (Birr, Co. Offaly) to Waterford was outlined thus:

Index No. of Railway	MC		Miles
12	Parsonstown to Maryboro'	37 77	
20	Maryboro' to Kilkenny	28 32	97½
20	Kilkenny to Waterford	31 0	

Down the line Clancy Barracks, formerly Islandbridge, can be spotted. We will get a closer look when we begin our journey, but from the military siding let us remember the commemorative tablet built into the north wall of an ordnance stores block. It does not honour a great general or even a gallant fusilier. Rather it tells that:

>Near this spot lie Buried, The Remains of
>DICKIE BIRD B.7
>Troop horse 5th Dragoon Guards
>Which was foaled in 1850
>Joined the Regiment in 1853

> And served throughout the entire Crimean Campaign
> From May 1854 to June 1856.
> He was shot on 21st Nov 1874
> By special authority from the Horse Guards
> To save him from being sold by auction.

Across in the Phoenix Park, the Wellington monument, a 205 foot phallic granite memorial to ducal conquests thrusts itself above tall trees. Its citation was composed by the duke's brother, Richard Wellesley:

> Asia and Europe, saved by thee, proclaim
> Invincible in war thy deathless name,
> Now round thy brow the civic oak we twine
> That every earthly honour may be thine.

That other protrusion above the park's foliage is the tower of the Royal Infirmary, now the headquarters of the Irish army.

But enough of this talk of war and conquest. There's an urgency about the modulated whine of the modern diesel-locomotive. Colmcille's 'fiery chariot' is no more and the only 'druidical deception' we are likely to come across travelling by Iarnród Éireann is a whimsical yarn told by a fellow traveller or a sprightly railwayman — like the one about the country squire who asked a station-porter about a consignment of small carrots he was loading. "Twas a poor crop this year,' said the porter, 'you could scrape them with a pencil parer.' Or the station master who gave the frightening piece of information that 'this train doesn't stop anywhere'. All aboard, then, for infinity!

Sit where you will, the blue and orange trim is inviting and a fine view can be got at both sides at once. The journey of 285 kilometres will take just over three hours.

Nosing out of the station, we reach Islandbridge, which once had its own pattern-day. St John's Well was the scene of merriment and entertainment on 23 June, the eve of the saint's feast-day. Clancy Barracks on the right is called after Peadar Clancy, a Clareman who was Vice-

Commandant of the Dublin Brigade of the IRA and who along with Dick McKee was tortured and killed when they refused to give information about Collins' 'Bloody Sunday' shootings (21 November 1920). Once it was an artillery barracks, later a hospital but now it is mainly a stores and workshop complex.

Nearby is the only salmon pool in the world where the coveted fish can be caught within the bounds of a capital city. The lease for this spot on the Liffey is very old. The neglected British Legion Memorial Park is alongside. Still moving slowly, we see on the left the vast maintenance and construction works for the railway at Inchicore, covering seventy-three acres in all. The fussy mock Tudor battlemented design was the idea of the Kingsbridge designer. In the days of the GS & WR it had its own school for railwaymen's children. Its highly skilled engineers turned out magnificent locomotives and coaches.

Goldenbridge, a short distance off, is now a large industrial estate. It was once a village in which Richmond Infantry Barracks and a military hospital were located. A Wesleyan Methodist meeting-house and school were erected here in 1835. Its 'Waterloo Spa' boasted 'sulphuretted hydrogen gas united with carbonic acid and magnesia' and was beneficial 'in bilious and liver complaints, scrobular and several other diseases'.[1]

Next we pass through Clondalkin on the River Camma. The Sancton Wood designed station is difficult to trace. Here was the country's largest paper-mill and the town's round tower was a distinctive feature in a trademark for quality Irish vellum. The Danes called the place Dun Awley and the Danish King of Dublin had his castle there until 806. St Cronan Mochua founded a monastery there and in 1171 Roderick O'Connor, King of Leinster, marched with the armies of O'Ruarc and O'Carroll but was repulsed by Strongbow at Clondalkin. A large number of prisoners were taken and today too the place is the site of Ireland's newest jail.

Leaving the city to merge in a hazy fusion with the backdrop of Dublin hills we cross the Griffen river at Grange. We have been heading west, but now a gradual bend brings the railway onto a west/south-west course which it will maintain until it reaches Portarlington. And after passing the remains of Hazlehatch station we are into the 'Short Grass' county. Kildare of the rich fertile plains, home of horse-racing and a hundred gamblers to every fool; a county still respected for its footballers, even though its heyday is long past. The track passes close to Castletown House, Celbridge. Built for William Connolly, speaker of the Irish House of Commons, it laid claim to being the largest private house in Ireland. Certainly its eighteenth century elegance has gained it the distinction of being the finest house and has established it as the headquarters of the Irish Georgian Society. The house itself cannot be seen, but a quick eye will detect 'Connolly's Folly', on the right. The obelisk-crowned arch was erected by Connolly's widow in 1740 as a relief scheme.

Kildare folklore cherishes the story of Connolly enjoying a stirrup-cup at a meet of the Kildare Hounds one morning. 'I'll ride against the devil to get the brush today,' he vowed. All day long the hunt roamed the coverts and fields and Connolly noticed a strange horseman riding alongside. No matter how fast he galloped he could not shake off the intruder. Both were right up with the hounds when the fox was caught. Connolly suggested drawing lots for the brush but the stranger declined; he insisted that Connolly should have it. Impressed by this, Connolly invited him to Castletown House where they dined lavishly and played cards cleverly. At one stage Connolly dropped a card, and stooping to pick it up he noticed his partner had a cloven foot.

To say that all hell broke loose would be appropriate as well as accurate! A flock of grey crows surrounded the house and terrified the staff. The parson was sent for but the devil only sneered at him. Connolly ordered the groom to get a priest but he refused. Eventually Connolly himself went for the curate in Celbridge. His return to Castletown was like Scarlet O'Hara's to Tara; the great mansion was on fire. He dashed in and was only just in time to shout bad cess to the 'auld boy' disappearing up the chimney.

Celbridge Hall, later Oakley Park, was built around 1724 for the vicar at Celbridge, Arthur Price. It was he who proposed to Dean Swift's 'Vanessa'. This lady, Esther Vanhomrigh, lived at Celbridge Abbey and a seat by the Liffey was their favourite courting place. On our left is Lyons House in whose demesne Daniel O'Connell is said to have fought a duel with an Orange member of Dublin Corporation named d'Esterre. O'Connell had denounced the older man as 'beggarly'. More reliable sources claim that the *affaire d'honneur* took place at Bishopscourt, near

Daniel O'Connell's duel with d'Esterre
Engraving from an Irish magazine, 1815

Naas. The location mattered little to d'Esterre — O'Connell shot him dead!

We gain momentum as we enter a long straight on top of an embankment. This is the place where, at 3 am on 31 March 1976, Ireland's 'Great Train Robbery' took place. An armed gang placed detonators on the line. Normally, these are a warning signal to train drivers, and when one of the raiders waved a red light on the track the driver drew to a halt. The man with the light boarded the engine and forced the driver to reverse to a spot where transport was waiting.

Meanwhile, in the mail compartment, post office officials had their sorting completed and were relaxing. Sacks of registered mail bore monies for fifty-seven Dublin banks and were clearly marked with red labels. Three masked men approached from the body of the train and took twelve of the bags; there was about £221,000 in them. The raid took a mere fifteen minutes.

Straffan station is just over a mile from the village and the house which in recent years was the location of an extravagant, star-studded party, lavishly hosted by Kevin McClory, the film director. There was nothing new in this, for in the eighteenth century John Joseph Henry married Lady Emily Fitzgerald, daughter of the Duke of Leinster. He was one of the wealthiest men of his time, yet his spendthrift ways forced him to sell Straffan House. Members of the family emigrated and made names for themselves in public life in Maryland, USA. A later resident, Hugh Barton, was a Bordeaux wine merchant. He used Straffan as an escape from a French purge of 1793-4 when foreign businessmen were cast into prison. He arranged for a partner, Daniel Guestier, to continue the business which has survived to this day. The B & G label is highly regarded by even the most fastidious palates.

Another member of the family, Robert Barton, was the longest surviving signatory of the Anglo-Irish treaty when he died in 1975. He was a member of the

Glendalough branch of the family. Ronald Barton was the latest representative of the Straffan Family at the Bordeaux concern. He served with the British and Free French forces during World War Two. The Germans occupied Chateau Léoville Barton. When informed that the establishment was Irish, they looted no cellars and damaged no property, though perhaps they did call for the bottle of Paddy whiskey hidden behind the Cuvée Thomas Barton!

Meals are being served on Iarnród Éireann now. Wonder does their wine cellar include Barton? Straffan was also the home of one of Ireland's most celebrated sportsmen, the motor-cyclist Stanley Woods. He won ten Tourist Trophy races in the Isle of Man.

Running a parallel course to the Royal Canal, the 'premier line' traverses the countryside of patriots. Over at Kill on the left, the Fenian leader John Devoy was born in 1842. As a young man he enlisted in the French Foreign Legion, and on his return he organised Fenians within the British Army. Later, he continued this work in the United States. It was he who steered the group who rescued six Fenian prisoners from Freemantle on board the *Catalpa* in a daring exploit.

Close to us on the right is Bodenstown:

> In Bodenstown churchyard there is a green grave,
> And wildly around it the winter winds rave.
> Small shelter, I ween are the ruined walls there
> As the storm sweeps down on the plains of Kildare.

The cemetery in which Wolfe Tone is buried is a place of annual pilgrimage for republicans of all shades. The ceremonies produce their quota of nationalists of convenience as well as genuine, sham and neo-patriots. Interred leaders are synonymous with this area because at nearby Blackhall was born the Revd Charles Wolfe, after whose family Tone was named and who wrote 'The Burial of Sir John Moore'. The poem tells of the death of a peninsular commander before the battle of Corunna:

> Not a drum was heard, not a funeral note,
> As his corpse to the ramparts we hurrried;
> Not a soldier discharged his farewell shot
> O'er the grave where our hero we buried.

Sallins has been the scene of many a muster and the march from the railway station to Bodenstown once was a *sine qua non* for those who would claim to wear the mantle of true republicanism. Nowadays, limousines and mighty words are adequate.

Some biographers of James Joyce say he came in a private car from Dublin to Clongoweswood College. Others claim that he travelled by train to Sallins, the nearest station to the school. Over a century earlier, in 1783, canal boats brought Volunteers from the city. They detrained at Sallins for a big review at the Curragh. The canal hotel opened a decade later near the tall building with the OTO (Odlum's Triumph Oatmeal) sign on the right. It was not a success and after eight years of trading it was offered for sale as a passage-boat stop. Eighteenth-century advertising copy-writers said of it: 'being in the neighbourhood of Mr Ponsonby's fox hounds renders it peculiarly eligible for any person wishing to engage in the tavern business.'[2] But a flour miller took over the lease in 1804 and the tradition lives on. Providing the staff of life is more enduring an enterprise than satisfying the needs of thirsty huntsmen!

During the 1798 rebellion, an officer and twenty men guarded Sallins canal bridge and there was still a 'Soldiers' Island' nearby when a railway bridge on the Naas branch held a pillbox and girder defences during World War Two.

Mention of Naas brings to mind the eighteenth-century practice of bull-baiting which took place at the Market Cross there. The early bloodsport was described by Archibald Hamilton Rowan of Rathcoffey (a few miles away) as:

> An innocent and manly amusement for the lower ranks of people [in which] a bull is procured, the wilder the better for the sport, and fastened to a stake by a rope about ten yards long in any commodious place. The spectators make a ring around him, the hardiest in the front, as their duty is when a dog is thrown up into the air, to run within the ring and by catching him to prevent him receiving any injury from the fall. The bull's horns seldom pierce the skin of the dog, but it frequently happens that men are hurt. Each person possessed of a dog brings him on a chain; there are never more than two, and generally one dog let on the bull at the time. Should a dog attack a bull anywhere but in front, he is taken up and turned out of the ring. That dog acquires the greatest favour who most frequently pins the bull, that is, seizes him by the upper lip, between the nostrils, and that man who has caught the most dogs has plainly been the most intrepid.[3]

At the end of the frolics, the bull was slaughtered and the flesh was distributed to the destitute. At the last baiting in Naas the beast tossed a cavalryman in the air and went berserk through the streets until it was stabbed in Basin Lane.

The pastime warranted a rousing ballad in Pat Connor's *Song Book*.[4] It stated:

> Myself, Pat O'Tullomagh came from Kildare.
> Whack, and old Erin, for ever, O!
> For jigging a lilt was the boy to a hair
> And at bull-baiting, monstrous clever, O!
> And arrah, and why not?
> 'Tis a way we have got
> To make the time pass away gaily, O.
> But, though Bulls, we avow,
> It isn't easy to cow
> The lads of the land of shilelah, O!

The canal and the Liffey are crossed and we are heading for Droichead Nua or Newbridge. Far right on the horizon we see Kildare's only claim to anything near a mountain. It is the Hill of Allen, with a tower perched on its summit. It looks intact but its rear is torn away for gravel and chips which are built into roads as far away as the United States. The bold Finn Mac Cumhaill exercised his Fianna around this hill and a tunnel is thought to connect it with Donadea Castle. It is said that if a human being crossed a certain stile between the two locations at the stroke of midnight, he would be transfixed. Now that's the sort of yarn to set the atmosphere for recalling a famous Kildare woman.

Close to the Hill of Allen there is a lesser slope, called the Hill of Grange. It is near a limestone outcrop known as the 'Chair of Kildare', but it is more renowned as the home of Moll Anthony. Most practitioners in the art of curing confined their cases to ailments of humans but '...the rale old Moll Anthony of the Red Hills...' seems to have had a veterinarian degree also. Moreover, she did not always attend at the farms of the sick beasts; once the animal's owner came to Moll, the beast was cured at the moment of consultation!

One of the many stories told about Moll is how a boy once met a funeral and, as was the custom, turned to walk some of the way behind the coffin, even helping to carry it. When the funeral came back to the boy's own gate the pall-bearers left down the coffin. The boy ran in to tell his mother and when they both came back out the coffin was still there but the mourners were gone. The lid was unscrewed and a young girl stepped from within. She lived with the family, taking the mother's name, Mary. When she and the boy, James, grew up, they married.

One day the young wife asked James to bring her with him to the fair in Castledermot. During the day an old farmer remarked to James that his bride was 'the spit' of his own daughter, buried many years before. The old farmer's wife agreed and quoted the date of their daughter's death. It coincided with the day James saw the girl step from the coffin. Mary even admitted it, for as the old farmer's wife ordered her to pull down the top of her dress she said, 'It's all right, mother; the raspberry mark is still on my shoulder'.

Those who held Moll Anthony to be in league with the 'good people', believed her to have been that girl, Mary (Moll). But this type of story rightly upsets some logical thinkers. Some of them claim that Moll Anthony's father was an Anthony Dunne and that she got her name because it was normal if a few families of the same name lived in an area, to use the father's christian name to distinguish his daughter.

Newbridge is the very heartland of gambling and football. These sporting inclinations were united for a brief glorious spell in the forties when a greyhound-racing track was laid about the Sarsfields GAA pitch to the horror of the Central Council of that body. A ban on foreign games was in force, you see, and the patriotism of dogs was open to question! Boldly the Kildare county team broke with tradition by interfering for the first time with their pristine strip. Emblazoned on their 'lily white' breasts during that championship season were defiant red hounds.

Larry Stanley, Matt Goff, Paul Doyle — great names from a glorious sporting past — drop from the lips here, as easily as fondly remembered horses like Tulyar, Brown Stout and another who was accused of hiding in furze bushes during a foggy Irish Grand National and popping out fresh and able to finish well ahead of the field next time around.

On the town's outskirts we notice the clock tower of the Dominican College on the left. That's where the sensitive and elegant sculptor, Fr Henry Flanagan worked some of his finest pieces. The College always had an eye for talent. James Joyce passed an Intermediate Examination in Belvedere in 1895. His results, particularly in science and mathematics, were less than spectacular. Indeed, he came last out of 164 to win a £20 scholarship, payable for three years. But two Dominican fathers called at his home offering a place at Newbridge. As it turned out, Joyce chose to remain in Jesuit care, at Clongoweswood.

Athlone-born Desmond Egan, a leading contemporary poet, teaches at Newbridge College too. He can encapsulate a gigantic series of tragic events in a few expertly chosen and crafted words, for example:

The Northern Ireland Question

> two *wee girls*
> were playing tig near a car...
>
> how many counties would you say
> are worth their scattered fingers?[5]

And it was an undistinguished edifice in Newbridge that inspired the lines of a lesser rhymester who courted a marvellous girl there back in the fifties:

The Cornerboy

> The shine has long been tarnished on Flynn's arch, sure.
> No leaning shoulders polish the sandstone.
> 'Tis said that affluence caused your departure —
> That you were lured by riches, but ochone!

Right well I know your noble mind shunned riches;
The reasons for your lingerings more sublime.
Your sad demise resulted from the stitches
That comely lasses chose to don in time.
Damned trouser-suits! they've caused Flynn's
    corner's clearance.
The staffs of life for cornerboys are limbs.
My proof lies in your welcome re-appearance
When mini-skirts fulfilled young damsels' whims.
But that was just a temporary fancy,
Your finest but your final hour, I fear.
And now you're gone forever from Kilclancey —
Unless those topless blouses should appear.
So, knickerbockers, parallels and trousers
Have killed you, chevalier cornerboy!
Good king of repartee and wit and rousers —
Alas! 'Le roi est mort, Vive le roi'.[6]

'The Back of the Ropes' in Newbridge, the rear wall of Irish Ropes, was a favourite place for young lovers to whisper terms of primitive endearment. There, fair maids from Athgarvan, Milltown or 'Borehard against the Wind', worked harder by day in 'the Cutlery' alongside.

    And straight I will repair, to the Curragh of Kildare
    'Tis there I'll find tidings of my love.

Ballymany, at the edge of the plains, is where the celebrated 'horsenapping' of Shergar took place. On the left, a short while after Newbridge, we see the flag-topped water tower of the Curragh Camp, Ireland's largest military establishment. Full of history, its most titled, if not the most revered, soldier was Edward VII who, as Prince of Wales, served there in 1861. He is said to have had a Dublin actress, Nellie Clifden, brought down by train and smuggled into his quarters. The education he received led him to use a certain VIP tunnel to 'Monto', the capital's red-light district, during his frequent visits to Ireland afterwards.

Charles Dickens, when he was a journalist, reported in the *Pall Mall Gazette* on camp-followers known as 'The Wren of the Curragh'. Unfortunate wretches came from backward places with their lovers and lived in appalling conditions. Their home was a warren burrowed into the earth and furze on mounds encircling the plains. Soldiers misappropriated vegetables, fuel and other commodities from army stores to help alleviate their misery. Some children were born and kept in the so-called 'wrens' nests'. When the cold winds penetrated the flimsy shelter of plaited gorse, women huddled together or took turns sitting on an upturned pot under which lighting coals were kept glowing by perforations in the metal. Scorned by the population, there were cases of priests horse-whipping the women and one drunken harridan emerged as the tyrannical leader of this most unusual group of bushwomen.

The grandstand of the home of the Budweiser Irish Sweeps Derby can be seen on the left. A 'Curragh siding' once brought racegoers by rail but it is no longer in use. The racing classics are part of a way of life in this area. Indeed it is alleged that a Mooretown girl once told a jockey that she would say a little prayer to St Leger for him!

The Curragh was once famous for another type of race — the Gordon Bennet motor-race. It first took place here in 1903 when English laws prevented road closure across the channel. It was the first occasion on which an American team participated in a European event. Camille Jenatzy of Germany won, driving a borrowed Mercedes at a startling 49.2 mph!

In Donnelly's Hollow was fought the famous fist fight between Dan Donnelly and George Cooper, in December 1815. We pass close to Gibbet Rath where, in 1798, 350 Irish rebels were slaughtered, even though they had surrendered. And Fr Moore's Well is also nearby on our right. It is different to many Irish wells in that it promises a cure for headaches provided the sufferer goes to a house close by and puts the priest's hat on his head.

But we are moving quickly and already Kildare town's 106 foot high round tower is beckoning on our left. Cill Dara, the Church of the Oaks, was St Brigid's foundation. The 'Mary of the Gael' was commemorated each year on her feast-day by making St Brigid's Crosses out of rushes and by parading 'The Breedogue'. This was an effigy made from a churn dash and was said to enhance the milk yield of the townlands through which it was carried.

St Brigid was promised some space for her monastery by a miserly landlord who told her to take as much land as her cloak would cover. She laid it on the ground and it spread and spread until it covered the Curragh. That's the legend, but Brigid's church became the principal one in Leinster and was before its time in that it was co-educational. Monks and nuns lived in separate cloisters, an abbot and an abbess co-ruled.

The Commander-in-Chief of the United Irishmen, Lord Edward Fitzgerald, lived here. Ireland's National Stud, with its unique equestrian museum and Japanese Gardens is at Tully, on the edge of the town. Its tiny bonsai trees and attractively landscaped arbours present the vicissitudes of man's life in oriental symbolism.

A Kildare woman was said to have been gaudily dressed and over made-up in Dublin's Bailey Restaurant and Bar one day when the poet, Paddy Kavanagh, was drinking there. An impatient man by normal standards, he was feeling particularly sore about something that day.

'You wouldn't ask me have I a mouth on me,' said the 'Short Grass' woman.

Kavanagh looked at her sourly and said, 'Why should I, miss, and it hanging between your ears like a skipping rope'.

But let us get back on the tracks! Revd Mr Baggot, a Kildare clergyman, was one of the first organisers of train excursions. Over 11,000 passengers travelled on them in one year alone. A Mr Thomas Cooke of Leicester followed suit, but in 1852 the railway company disallowed his credit.

With the town of Brigid behind us, we notice Cherryville junction where a line to Athy, Carlow, Kilkenny and Waterford branches. Best forgotten is the serious accident there on 21 April 1983. Eight people were killed and thirty injured, but the disaster might have been far worse, since up to 500 passengers, mostly children, were aboard the trains.

Some forest plantations are apparent here but when note is taken of the huge amount of marshy ground in the central plain through which we are travelling, it seems shameful that trees do not dominate the landscape.

Note also a small town with two conspicuous and attractive churches. This is Monasterevin, meeting place of canal, railway, highway and the noble river Barrow. The long viaduct that bears us across is known as 'Hellfire Jack's Bridge'. That's because the driver of the first steam train to cross it, when it opened in 1840, shouted, 'Now, for hell or Cork'. Ireland's most renowned singer and arguably the world's greatest lyric tenor, John McCormack, lived occasionally at Moore Abbey between 1924 and 1936. Monsignor Fulton Sheen and Gene Tunney visited him there. Representatives of the 'Victor Talking Machine Company' for whom he cut nearly 200 records were also regular attenders at the gracious home. Today, the Sisters of Charity lovingly treat epileptic and other cases there.

The town gets its name from St Evin, who hailed from Cashel and was the legendary son of Eoghan Mór (Big John), who fathered the Munster Eoghanacht. During solemn trials, the tribe swore oaths upon the bell of St Evin. A clanger was dropped if a false promise was made upon it; the bell leaped in the air, and could well fall on the perpetrator. Particularly perturbed by a sixth-century perjurer, it hopped so high that it dropped into the river Figile and was never found.

Monasterevin was also well-known for the production of alcoholic drinks:

Alas, alas poor whiskey,
That spirit pure and clear,
Which made its drinker frisky
Yet left his liver clear.
How vile adulterations
Have caused its name to stink,
Can Irishmen be traitors
To Ireland's noblest drink?

A family by the name of Cassidy once owned a distillery in the town. In addition, they had the authority to save one person from the gallows each year. During the 1798 rebellion, a certain Fr Prendergast was sentenced to be hanged, so he sent word to the distillers, seeking a reprieve. They refused. Before he died, it was said that the cleric placed a curse on the family, vowing that crows would soon be building nests in the malt-houses and that nobody named Cassidy would be left living in Monasterevin. In 1886, however, the poet Gerard Manley Hopkins declared a Miss Cassidy of the brewing family to be 'one of the props and struts of his existence'.[7] From

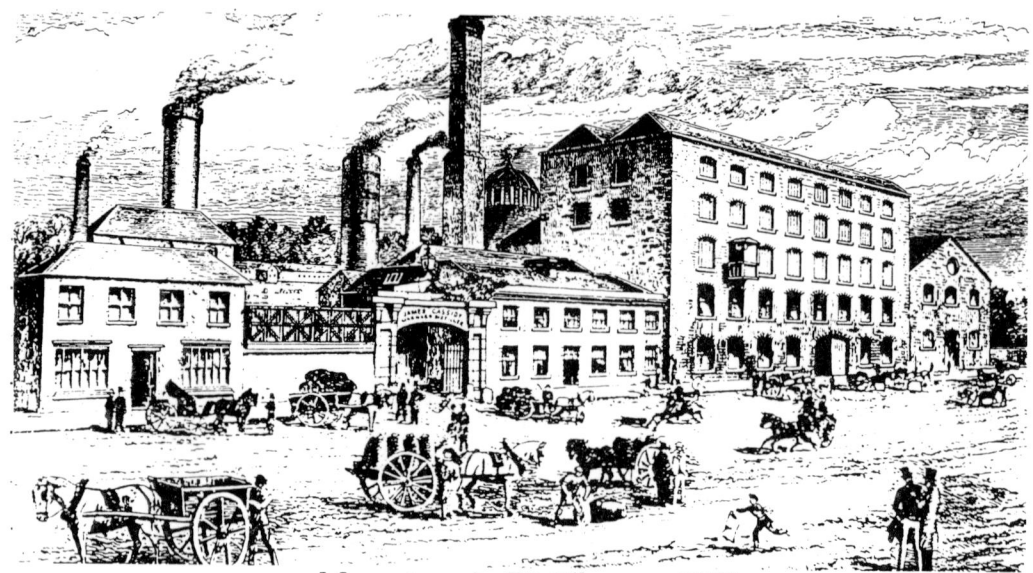

Monasterevin Distillery, c. 1887

Monasterevin too he forwarded at least one sonnet to the poet/publisher, Robert Bridges. And it was only in 1921 that the distillery closed, after 140 years of business. 'The Curse of the Cassidys' was tardy in reaching fruition.

In more recent times the town was subject to world media exposure during the Herrema case. Two kidnappers holding the Dutch industrialist were surrounded in a Monasterevin housing estate and were kept under siege for sixteen days before they surrendered and their victim was freed.

CHAPTER 3

CO. LAOIS

Shortly after Monasterevin we cross into County Laois, known previously as Queen's County. Ancient 'Leix' corresponded with the old diocese of Leighlin. Laoghis Réta was O'Moore's territory; it covered an area around Portlaoise (Maryboro'). The county's regal associations gave its inhabitants a certain grandeur. It is interesting to note that after the opening of the new Lying-In Hospital (the Rotunda) in Dublin in 1756, there was a 'Queen's County Bed', with an inscription to that effect in gold letters. It was to be used only by Laois women. The High Sheriff and Grand Jury voted £26.14s.7½d. towards it, making Queen's County the only one outside Dublin so represented. Coal-mining and fire-clays, footballing and hurling are associated with modern Laois. An old *pisogue* says they will never win an All-Ireland Championship title while there is a Delaney on the team. Yet they came closest when they fielded three Delaney brothers! Their superstitions must be as impotent as neighbouring Kildare's curses!

Portarlington is now at hand. We can recognise the town by the cooling tower of its peat-fired power-station — the country's first. Above and beyond stretch the great midland bogs — Derrylea, Clonsast and the sprawling Bog of Allen. They produce millions of tonnes of turf and peat products each year.

A pleasant station-house and metal crossover bridge are features of the architecture at this junction for the west of Ireland. It may have been here that an early passenger, an English literature professor, heard a porter rattling off his instruction:

'Changehereforathlonegalwayandmayo.'

Portarlington Power Station

Loading of Sod Peat

The cold, calculated murder of the language's punctuation shocked the eminent scholar, so he chastised the perpetrator saying: 'You must sing out the names clearly and distinctly.' Next time he used the line, he heard the porter actually singing the verse:

> Sweet dreamland faces
> Passing to and fro,
> Change here for Athlone
> Galway and Mayo.[8]

Called after Lord Arlington, the town had, until comparatively recently, a French Huguenot colony. In the eighteenth century they gained for the place a name for fine silverwork, by fashioning a mace for Portarlington. The artefact is now displayed at London's Goldsmiths' Hall. Moreover, the town's La Touche family helped to develop banking in Ireland. Indeed, this cosmopolitan population also produced a distinctive horticulture and a 1722 bill of deeds for plants, etc., from the Hague included:

> Lemon or citron trees, turnep seed, mhirtle balls in pots, esparagus, sencitive plants, several sorts of latices, and about 60 sorts of flower seeds, raadishes, and ramolas.

Past Cúl an tSúdaire, we see on the left a prominent tree-covered hill with a spire protruding. This is of no significance except as a spur of the wooded area south, which is Emo Court, the Earl of Portarlington's (John Dawson) Gandon-designed seat. Now a Jesuit novitiate, this Irish house of neo-classical elegance has works of art by Oisin Kelly, Eric Hone and others.

Still further south is 'The Great Heath of Maryboro'. At its southern extremity, in Ballydavis, was an Irish phenomenon known as a 'swally hole'. A gushing stream of water flowed into a hole in the earth, and so it 'swallied' humans (especially bold children, parents threatened) who were foolish enough to step into it. Moy

Réta, the plain of Riata, was the ancient name of 'The Heath'.

On the right we see the Ridge of Capard, northernmost feature of the great Slieve Bloom range which will dominate the horizon for a while. We enter a deep ravine before Portlaoise. This is part of 'The Ridge of Maryboro' or the Portlaoise Esker, the country's longest at 14 kilometres. After emerging, if we look left and back we can get a glimpse of the distinctive Rock of Dunamase in the distance. Dermot McMurrough, King of Leinster, gave this keep to his daughter Aoife as a dowry for her marriage with Strongbow. Centuries later, in 1641, Sir Charles Coote seized it for the O'Moores. Eoghan Roe O'Neill recaptured it in 1646 but four years later the castle came under Cromwellian attacks and was destroyed. This incident is recalled by historians who point out 'Cromwell's Lines ' and his gun platform.

A clothier of Oliver's army called Daniel Byrne, was invited to dinner at Shean Castle, an outpost of Dunamase. He was not supplied with a knife so he praised his host, Whytney of Shean, for the abundance of good meat, but complained of having nothing with which to cut it. He was told bluntly, 'Why don't you draw out your scissors and cut it to measure your mouth'. A rhyme celebrates the incident:

> Dan Byrne could tailor uniforms for Cromwell's
>   dastard force
> His Irish friends disliked him for his trade.
> When dined at Whytney's castle he was served a
>   splendid course
> Of ox-meat, tripe, fried leeks and marmalade.
> Not wishing to be impolite a knife he did request,
> To cut his cow in cubes before he ate.
> His host despised such arrogance from his artisan
>   guest
> And told Dan Byrne to take his flaming plate
> And bring it to the inglenook, then lay it on
>   the slab;

Rock of Dunamase, Co. Laois

> Dan did as he was bid.'Now what?' asked he;
> 'Your scissors take, and cross your legs like some
>   paralysed crab,
> And evermore display servility.'

But let us away from this area with its social climbing tailors and horsemen in knightly garb who, we are told, head a procession of carriages bearing elegantly clad ladies on a ghostly parade across 'The Heath'.

Portlaoise was called Maryboro' in honour of Queen Mary I (Mary Tudor, 1516-68), whose persecution of Protestants earned her the title 'Bloody Mary'. After marrying Philip II of Spain, she reduced the rich land around the town to shire ground, by act of parliament. As we have already noted, the county was called Queen's County, and neighbouring Offaly was King's County with Philipstown (now Daingean) its capital.

As we near the station, the first things we notice on the left are a war memorial and Portlaoise prison with its lookout posts on top; it is a high security jail. A publication titled *In Maryboro' and Mountjoy* by 'An Irish Priest'[9] tells how, in the aftermath of Thomas Ashe's death on hunger strike in 1917:

> A special cell was prepared in Portlaoise for troublesome political prisoners who refused to wear prison garb. A false ceiling allowed a warder to spy from above, while a powerful radiator ensured that pneumonia wouldn't develop. 'Muffs' constituted a severe form of punishment. An arrangement of leather flaps and straps by which all the trunk of the body, the arms and hands, were so tightly bound as practically to paralyse all play of tendons and muscles.

The standard strait-jacket in use in mental institutions at the time was considered mild by comparison. The wearing of prison garb by political prisoners is a controversial issue to this very day.

An acclaimed hanging took place in Portlaoise in August 1735. Charles O'Dempsey, known as Cahir-na-gCapall, stole horses and dyed them with a substance made from alum and brazilette boiled in water. His own steed had its shoes nailed on back to front to deceive persistent, pursuing peelers. There was no sympathy for Cahir, because horse-thieving was regarded as a despicable crime.

Passengers in the front coaches will notice, when the train stops, the premises on the left with Ptk Kelly & Co. in bold letters. This firm was known all over rural Ireland in pre-war years when they built haybarns and other farm outhouses. There is a pleasant little church nearby and the townscape displays signs of wool and milling traditions.

The railway reached Portlaoise in June 1847. Its cost? — £3,000 per mile. A line to Abbeyleix operated between 1867 and 1962 and detailed plans still exist in the National Library of Ireland for seven miles, four furlongs and six chains of a 'Maryborough and Stradbally Tramway'. They were drawn up in 1883. A proposed connection to

Mullingar reached Mountmellick in 1885. It also closed in 1962.

When we leave Portlaoise we notice areas of bogland, particularly on the right. Some of its produce is covered with plastic to give the impression of being a great lake. We speed past Mountrath, which is well inland on the right. The train cannot stop because only a platform remains. Yet Mountrath once had a thriving linen industry, fostered by Sir Thomas Coote. Its affluence may have inspired the limerick:

> There was an old dame from Mountrath,
> Who grew ten times too big for her bath.
> Then one winter, alas,
> She ate nothing but grass.
> Now she's greenish but thin as a lath.

The verse may serve to cheer, for we are passing through drab, unpleasant country saved only by the persistence of the undulating mass of the Slieve Blooms. Fernand Braudel, a French geographer, said that 'the history of mountain areas is that they have no history', but what this range lacks in history it makes up for in ecology:

> Sliabh Bladhma caomh os a chionn
> Osraidhe, ós ardaibh Eirionn...
> Ní bréag, ó Bhearnán Eile
> Go Conlán-chin-sen-t-sléibhe,
> Sliabh Bladhma ar fad is é sin,
> Gárda é a n-am lag Laighen.
>
> (Ó Huaidhrin)

Archaeological finds in the Blooms are of Neolithic and Bronze Age and some fossil spores discovered in the Silurian rocks of the great Ridge of Capard are the oldest ever unearthed. The wild goats that roam them, tread on ancient soil.

Up there is the highest peak of central Ireland. If climbed by a bright-eyed adventurer on a clear day, Arderin, 'the

Height of Ireland', affords a view to the south as far as Waterford's Comeragh mountains and to Galway's Twelve Pins in the west; south-west to Kerry, east to Wicklow and Dublin — a third of the country altogether. Yet, from Iarnród Éireann's fast moving coach, Arderin's 526 metres looks almost insignificant.

Welsh traveller Geraldus Cambrensis spoke of a well 'in Munster' and said, 'I saw a man who had washed there one part of his beard. It had turned grey, while the other part retained its natural dark colour'. But a Norse chronicle, used by Geraldus, placed the well in the Slieve Blooms. The eleventh century *De Mirabilibus Hiberniae (The Wonders of Ireland)* says:

> Cernitur a multis alius fons more probatus,
> Qui facit ut dicunt canos mox esse capillos.
>
> Another duly proven well is known
> That quickly greys one's hair.

Ballybrophy station still stands, despite acrimonious threats. Nearly nine kilometres away on the right, upon the branch line to Roscrea and Limerick is Borris-on-Ossory. It was there, and not at Ballybrophy, that a station was envisaged originally. Its traders objected, thinking it would have an adverse effect on their business.

Ballybrophy has the dubious distinction of being the location for Ireland's first railway homicide. 'Milesmen' were maintenance labourers who were allowed to harvest hay on a portion of the embankments as part of their remuneration. They hauled their saved cocks home on railway bogeys. They fried rashers and eggs on their broad shovels over open fires by the side of the permanent way. One of them, John D'Arcy, was accused of killing one Michael Smith by striking him on the left side of the head 'with a stone of no value'.[10] Perhaps we are to assume that, had the stone been valuable, his sentence of death might have been more severe! That's what was meted out to him when, after a period spent in the army in Cork under an assumed name, he was executed at Ballybrophy on 23 March 1848.

As we move on, watch out for a large quarry on the left. This is Lisduff and it has a special significance because Córas Iompair Éireann and its predecessors quarried its stone for use on the permanent underlay for track and sleepers. Comhlucht Siúicre Éireann (the Irish Sugar Company) quarried for lime here also. If conditions are right when passing, the dark grey and black limestone may be seen. A feature of the shale partings on Lisduff Hill is their dark grey oolites (egg stones) shaped like tiny fish eggs. The core of each of these is a minute sand or shell particle. A station here was closed to passenger traffic in 1963.

A man from Erril was sticking gummed labels on luggage at Lisduff many years ago when a posh local landlord arrived on the platform to catch the Dublin train. He studied the porter for a while before asking, 'Don't you keep a brush for that work?'

The Erril porter replied, 'No, your honour, our tongues is the only instruments we're allowed — but they're easily kept wet!'

CHAPTER FOUR

CO. TIPPERARY

Lisduff's stones remind us of the 'Tipperary Stone-Throwers' and sure enough we enter Ireland's largest inland county soon after. The Galtees and Knockmealdowns unite in different parts to isolate Slievenamon and Keeper's Hill but the whole shire is a scenic, fertile land:

> Ah sweet is Tipperary in the springtime of the year
> When the hawthorn's whiter than the snow;
> When the feathered folk assemble, and the air is all a-tremble
> With their singing and their winging to and fro.
> When queenly Slievenamon, keeps her verdant vesture on
> And smiles to hear the news the breezes bring.
> When the sun begins to glance on the rivulets that dance
> Ah sweet is Tipperary in the spring.

Whiteboyism flourished here because of a dense population, and a great greed for land. And because that land was good, less effort was required to work it, so idle hands turned to criminal acts. Illicit distilling was once prevalent in the county; this too made the crime rate soar. A rhyme ridiculing common Tipperary names went:

> All Ryans are rogues,
> All Dwyers cut-throats
> All O'Donnells root the ditches
> All Moroneys lick the dishes.

'Tipperary' was a famous war song but that very fact inspired modern people of goodwill there to establish a vigorous peace movement. However, Ireland's War of Independence began in Tipperary when two members of the Royal Irish Constabulary were shot dead at Soloheadbeg on the day the first Dáil sat, 21 January 1919.

But today, peaceful grazing cows do not even lift their heads as we pass. We see hedges of blackthorn, whitethorn and ash — used for the *camán* (hurley stick), a respected instrument in 'Tipp'. Indeed most of our route on the 'premier line' is through prime hurling country — Laois, Tipperary, Limerick and Cork.

There have been few signs so far of the rich, fertile land for which the county is celebrated. But then railway builders used flatlands, and in Ireland, flat is wet. Since we are travelling with Iarnród Éireann we must note this county's close associations with the beginning of public transport. In 1808, Charles Bianconi took a corner shop in Clonmel to run a small business. By 1815, the end of the Napoleonic wars and a tax on carriages made it easy to buy up horses and so he set up his famous road-car (Bian) service with a trip to Cahir. By 1864 his service covered 4,000 miles of road. When railways were introduced he did not offer any opposition. Indeed, he invested in them before retiring — in Tipperary, of course, under the shadow of the Rock of Cashel.

The Tannoy delivers the message that the next stop is Templemore.

Quickly! Look to the right. Notice, near the left of that dark, treacherous ridge of mountains, a distinct gap. That's the Devil's Bit. At least that's what it's called. The Devil's Bit mountain is to its right but to the Gap of Eile alongside is given the title. That's because, you see, the devil was hungry one day and the good Tipperary Christians had refused him sustenance, despite threats of transportation to Cork! So Satan bit a lump out of the mountain. More used to brimstone and hot curries, he found it unpalatable and spat it out again. It landed twenty miles away and formed the pile that is now the Rock of Cashel. A pity that unromantic geologists spoil this tale by certifying that Bearnán Eile (the Gap of Eile — the Devils' Bit) cuts through sandstone while Cashel's base is limestone. Up there in a mountain cave was found, in 1790, a manuscript copy of the Gospels. It was written in Latin using ancient Irish calligraphy of thirteenth century origin.

There is a stop at Templemore (An Teampall Mór — the Big Church), although its station buildings are not impressive. The 'goods yard' is very busy though, due, no doubt, to the wealth of this fertile countryside.

The training depot for recruits to An Garda Síochána is in Templemore, but a former police-force was involved in an incident here which became known as 'The Bleeding Statues'.

Back in the time of Ireland's 'Troubles', the local police barracks was garrisoned by Black and Tans and there were several shootings in the area in 1920. After the funeral of a district inspector in the town, Mr Dwan, a newsagent, was visited by a certain James Walsh from Curraheen, a seventeen-year-old youth who announced that he was about to reveal a message to the world. A frail, gentle lad, Walsh was reported to have studied for the priesthood and was known to speak with great enthusiasm about spiritual things. Mr Dwan's sister employed him as a farm labourer.

James had mentioned to Mr Dwan that he was visited by the Blessed Virgin, who registered her disapproval of the way Irish society was becoming sinful; she asked James to voice her feelings abroad. She also asked him, he said, to scrape a hole in the earthen floor of his cottage which stood at the foot of the Devil's Bit. When he obeyed, water filled the hole and soon it became a clear-running well. Whenever the Lady visited him, a statue in the cottage bled.

James claimed to have been visited during the previous night when the town was ransacked by Black and Tans, eager to avenge the district inspector's death. The Lady told Walsh that only through her intervention had the soldiers been restrained from destroying the town completely.

Mr Dwan helped James place a small table in the yard behind the newsagency. A white cloth was laid on this and three of Walsh's statues were put standing on it. The blue and white gown on each image was splashed by a bloodstain which began at the face and trickled down. A crippled man came to the table and was seen later that day throwing away his crutches and running down the street, followed by an ecstatic crowd who shouted praise to God while claiming a miracle. A local RIC sergeant vouched for the truth of the account.

Next day, the newspapers carried the story and people from all over Ireland began converging on Templemore. More and more cures were claimed, and rules in force at the time forbidding motorists from travelling more than twenty miles without a permit had to be abandoned. It was said that the IRA, against whom the regulation had been established, moved men on the run, supplies, ammunition and provisions during the fortnight of the bleeding statues.

And it lasted no longer than that. It is on record that a member of the RIC bought one of the statues and kept it in his kit-box in the barracks. Word spread that a peeler owned a statue and crowds called at the barracks demanding a blessing. They were kept at bay until the Sunday after the 'revelation' when a woman who had come from Donegal with her deformed child, could no longer stand the long wait in the queue outside Dwans'. She had been travelling all Saturday night and she begged the police to admit her. They did so and she was left alone in the barrack-room with her child before the statue. When she came out, a mob had gathered and were calling for admission. A perplexed garrison was saved only by the arrival of the Divisional Commissioner for Munster who took the sacred object, stood outside the barrack-gate, holding it while the crowd passed by touching it and praying. Armed Auxiliaries and Tans stood guard. It was a remarkable sight.

Remarkable too was the fact that soldiers, Black and Tans and all sorts of odd people began seeking instruction in the Catholic faith from Templemore's clergy. The shooting and the destruction ceased and the town took on a carnival air as the crowds of pilgrims grew as fast as the heap of crutches in Walsh's yard.

The routine was: a visit to the statues at Dwans', followed by a trip out to Walsh's to drink the water from the well. The clergy did not recognise the alleged phenomena, although a few of their younger men helped pilgrims. A cockney soldier vowed that he saw a 'lydy' in blue and the townsfolk swore that they would erect a statue on the spot where he was afforded the privilege of being granted an apparition. Business boomed in Templemore. Visitors and reinforcements for the harassed police swelled the coffers of the merchants.

Then, almost as suddenly as it began, the whole thing ended. The affair had lasted a little over two weeks. People were as baffled by the sudden end as they had been at the beginning. There were tales of the flow of water in the 'well' being helped. And the movement of the local IRA from the town to safety, away from the Tans, clamouring for revenge after the inspector's death, was achieved.

Many other stories have been whispered into foam-topped tumblers down the years but there has never been a completely satisfactory explanation of Templemore's bleeding statues.

Templemore was always a major railway station, a company storage workshop and distribution depot. Railway-coach window straps were once greatly sought after from the repair workshops at Thurles. Barbers and owners of 'cut throat' razors found they made excellent strops. And some were even pilfered *en route* by nimble-fingered barbers. This verse appeared in *Punch* magazine:

> Gentlemen you rarely meet
> Hiding underneath your seat.
>
> Though we smash you into bits,
> Never mind — you've brought 'Short-Skits'.

Leave the window straps behind
Other razor strops you'll find.

On our buns bruise not your fists
Leave them to geologists.

Thurles is the cathedral town of the archdiocese of Cashel and Emly. Strongbow's Anglo-Norman force, assisted by settlers from their colony in Dublin, was defeated here by Roderick O'Connor and Donal O'Brien. But the Anglo-Normans later established themselves and erected a castle in order to command the crossing of the Suir.

Today, the most dominant feature of the townscape is the spire of St Patrick's seminary. The National Synod of 1850 took place here; it proscribed the Queen's Colleges and authorised a Catholic university at Dublin which Dr (later Cardinal) John Henry Newman founded four years later.

When the vigorous nationalist, Dr Thomas Croke (1824-1902) was archbishop, he joined Charles Stewart Parnell and Michael Davitt as patrons of the fledgeling Gaelic Athletic Association. Indeed, a letter of his, supporting the movement, has often been referred to as the 'charter of the GAA'. The association's headquarters in Dublin, Croke Park, is named in his honour. And it all began at Hayes' Hotel in Thurles on 1 November 1884. Present at the foundation meeting were Michael Cusack, teacher; Maurice Davin, athlete; John Wyse Power, Fenian; P. J. Ryan, solicitor; John McKay, journalist; John R. Bracken, builder and George McCarthy, district inspector, RIC. Even today many enthusiasts regard a Munster Hurling Final at Thurles as the single greatest national sporting event.

This area is also associated with William Smith O'Brien, a leading member of the Young Irelanders and co-founder of the 1847 Irish Confederation which embarked upon an ill-prepared armed rising the following year. O'Brien led a small armed party which clashed with close on fifty policemen in the cabbage garden of the Widow McCormack at Ballingarry, about seventeen kilometres to our left behind the Slieveardagh hills. This ignominious skirmish, a favourite topic in Irish-American conversation, ended the 1848 rebellion.

Shortly afterwards, on 5 May, an English employee of the L & NWR, William Hulme by name, was instructing native railwaymen in their duties at Thurles station. By a pre-arranged signal, he pointed out O'Brien and the police moved in and manhandled him as they took him into custody. Anger swept the area and the military were sent into the streets to contain O'Brien's supporters in their homes, while the patriot was being marched off to the bridewell. Later that day, a train was commandeered to

Arrest of William Smith O'Brien at Thurles Railway Station in 1848, taken from the *Illustrated London News*

bring him under heavy escort to Kilmainham Jail. Hulme received a handsome reward and returned to England where he purchased a public hostelry. He was its best customer, apparently, because he died of alcoholic poisoning shortly afterwards.

> Oh hear ye the song of the two famous Bills
> One was Hulme and the other, O'Brien.
> One fought for old Ireland on Munster's green hills,
> Till a peeler discovered him lyin'
> In wait in a cabbage-patch, warlike and bold;
> His comrades astride Spanish onions
> With pitchforks held high, two and twenty all told
> And a small Dundrum dwarf who had bunions.
>
> Bill Hulme knew this leader, and a girl from
>   Goold's Cross,
> Said she'd give him whatever he fancied
> If he'd show Smith O'Brien to her grandfather's boss –
> A policeman all poppish and gansied.
> This plain clothes galoot, I will tell you the truth,
> On the permanent way stood one morning,
> Gathering ha'pennies galore as he tootled a flute
> For the passengers under the awning.
>
> Then bold Hulme nods his head, and the peeler instead
> Of his flute, blew a note on his whistle
> From the men's waiting-room came a squadron led
> By a chief who looked like a bent thistle.
>
> These men fell on O'Brien, knocked him down on the line.
> And they charged him with bold insurrection.
> While Bill Hulme took reward and crossed over the brine
> In a dastardly, cunning defection.
>
> With his ill-gotten gains he did purchase an inn
> But the guardians of good, they were winking
> For the infamous wretch spent his whole time within,
> And he rotted his liver from drinking.

On the left, leaving Thurles, one of the country's large sugar factories can be seen. Beyond, on the horizon, are the Slieveardagh hills again. In between is rich, productive soil, part of the Golden Vale. Littleton is in there with its monastic site founded by St Ruadhán. The unfortunate saint was better known for putting a curse on Tara and for having a tree upon which food grew. That deciduous dining-plant flourished in his parent abbey at Lorragh, many kilometres to the north-west, and forgotten. But the Littleton site has leaped to world prominence as Derrynaflan, where in 1980, the acclaimed Derrynaflan chalice and paten were discovered by a father and son, using a metal detector.

To the horror of archaeologists, Ireland's High Court ruled initially that the finders were owners of the five million pound treasure. The grave of a legendary Irish character, the *Gobán Saor* — a mighty mason— is at Derrynaflan also. It was desecrated shortly after the judgement on the Derrynaflan hoard was given. If the *Gobán's* lump-hammer was found nobody has yet sought a reward!

The River Suir is close to us on the left as we pass under and then move parallel to a main road. The next village on the left is Holy Cross. In 1908, 300 members of the RIC were hurried by rail to deal with a disturbance caused by evicted tenants here. Many centuries earlier it seems, four robbers assaulted a destitute hermit. They demanded certain treasure which they believed he possessed, and threatened that they would kill him if he failed to hand it over. They could not be convinced that the holy man was what he claimed. Eventually, they suggested that if such was the case, he should bring about a miracle.

'Have that old tree there bow to us', they sneered.

The hermit would not ask God; he had more respect for his deity than to call for assistance when there was nothing at stake but his own humble life. But, of its own accord, the

Derrynaflan Chalice

tree did a dignified curtsey. When the quartet of rogues went to examine the phenomenon, their hands stuck to its branches and it immediately sprang back into an upright position. Just then the King of Thomond, Donal Mór O'Brien, rode by. He heard the hermit's tale and in a fit of rage he cut down the robbers from their leafy suspension by slashing through their wrists with his sword. Thus *Ochtar Lamha* (eight hands) was the original name of the village that now boasts a celebrated and architecturally beautiful Cistercian monastery. Holy Cross Abbey has undergone restoration towards which the state contributed 25 per cent of the cost.

The story of the old hermit was depicted graphically in an old parchment book titled *Triumphalia Cronologica*, found at Holy Cross parish church in 1752. But it is almost certain that an abbey existed there since the twelfth century.

A relic called 'The Holy Rood' brought fame to the place. One story concerning its origin tells how a prince known as 'The Good Woman's Son' was collecting tithes for the Vatican, commonly called 'Peter's Pence'. He was set upon by thieves in a copse near the holy place, and was killed in the ensuing struggle. The robbers buried him under a tree but a blind monk from the abbey was guided by an unexplained vision to the spot. Driven by some preternatural force, he exhumed the corpse and took the prince's ring from it. He brought it over to England and presented it to his mother. In her gratitude she granted the relic of the Holy Rood to Holy Cross!

Up to 20,000 worshippers per day have been known to attend the abbey's 'Festival of Faith', a solemn novena held in recent years. The relic, venerated in the north trancept, is an authenticated acquisition from St Peter's Basilica in Rome, and has no romantic lore attached to it.

A prominent, lone, wooded hill in the left centre distance, is called Killough Hill. It is mentioned only as a landmark because we are now speeding through the Suir Valley, where we soon flash past Goold's Cross. This was once important handballing country and mention of the game reminds us of Matt the Thresher in Charles Kickham's *Knocknagow*, subtitled 'The Homes of Tipperary'. Goold's Cross station is closed and deserted; it is hard to believe that over in Cashel, an elaborate fountain was erected just eighty years ago (1904) in recognition of the part played by that town's parish priest (Very Revd Joseph Mary Kinane) in bringing about an extension railway line from Goold's Cross which opened in that year. Six round-trips were made daily, taking a mere fifteen minutes each way. Among the considerable mail and freight were fifteen churns of cream which went all the way to Paddington, thus bringing rich Golden Vale produce to fine Mayfair tables. An annual outing from Cashel to Dublin, via Goold's Cross, was called the 'Blackberry Express'. Goold's Cross itself once displayed a notice, declaring it the 'Station for Rockwell College'. Near Cashel, this institution once had Eamon de Valera as its professor of mathematics (1903).

We see a horseshoe of heights ahead. The Galtee mountains above the famed Glen of Aherlow rise in the left foreground; assorted folds offer variety on the right. Notice a large wooded area there. That's Rasheen and opposite on our left is Dundrum, the village after which the celebrated Irish show-jumper ridden by a famous son, Tommy Wade, was called.

A story is told about an American tourist driving a huge Cadillac saloon into Dundrum village in the mid-thirties. He halted at a petrol pump — one of the old pre-electricity types operated by pumping a handle back and forward. His tank was nearly empty so he requested a fill up. He left the car engine running while he hopped into a nearby shop to buy cigarettes. The petrol pump attendant, an elderly man who had a bronchial complaint, began pumping. Harder and harder he worked but there was no sign of the petrol reaching the top of the tank. He wheezed and puffed and perspired as he sped up his strokes and pumped harder and harder. Still the tank wasn't filled so he stopped, went to the shop and called to the American:

'Would you ever come back and switch this thing off. I think it's catching up on me!'

Now the countryside is becoming more interesting, but just as we begin to admire it we slide into a long cutting. When we re-emerge, the scene is desolate; we seem to be lost in a coarse, wild scrubland. Adding to the Beckettian aspect is a shorn telegraph pole, its wires hanging down

Tommy Wade on Dundrum

like a banshee's tresses. Its dozens of lines are replaced by a single multicore cable.

A Tipperaryman once took over planting those same poles from a Kerryman. At nightfall he went to the foreman and told him he had sunk twenty poles. 'But the Kerryman was able to erect thirty poles each day,' said the foreman, and the stone-thrower replied, 'Sure he did; but did you see how much of them he left sticking up?'

After crossing the Multeen river we begin slowing down for a stop at Limerick Junction. The race-course is visible on the right; lucky passengers might even see a horse-race on the course now called 'Tipperary'.

Palm trees grow alongside the station buildings here, indicating a milder climate than the midlands through which we have passed. Railway enthusiasts love to come here to witness the busy shunting and other operations. Terms clear only to themselves and the railway employees include a 'red-lamp area', a 'cripple siding', and trains known as the 'soup', the 'perishable' or 'crawler' and the 'flying saucer'.

The people of Limerick were always anxious to make sure that the railway would reach them. Its Town Council monitored the progress of the Dublin and Cashel Railway Bill through parliament, vowing to 'devise and adopt such measures as may appear necessary to secure the continuation of the railroad to the Cities of Limerick and Cork.'[11]

When the Waterford and Limerick Railway (W & LR) began operating between the cities in 1848, a ceremony was held at Limerick Junction. Lord Clarendon, the Viceroy, attended, along with assorted titled and ranked gentlemen and the directors of the railway. There were demonstrations as they passed through Templemore on a special train. Word went ahead and a wily official paid railway workers at the Junction one shilling per head if they agreed to clap the arrival of the gentry. The *Freeman's Journal* did not think they gave value for money. It reported that they gave 'a real Tipperary cheer' when someone called for it on behalf of the recently arrested Young Irelander, John Mitchel, but 'one of the most consumptive cheers ever heard' for the Viceroy. There was a banquet in Lord Hawarden's seat at Dundrum and the carousers returned to Dublin by train late that night.

Winston Churchill was very late arriving at the Junction once. Having left Dublin hours before and having endured long delays at all stations, he was impatient when requested to change for Tralee. He boarded the train bound for the Kerry capital and he waited – and waited! He lost his temper then, stuck his head out the window and called to the guard, 'I am Winston Churchill', and went on to explain how he had an important appointment with Lord Kenmare. Then he demanded that the train should start moving. The guard crooked a finger and beckoned him out onto the platform. He tugged at Sir Winston's elbow and guided him down past the engine. Pointing at the signal, he said to Churchill, 'Do you see that yoke? Well, when it's down like that, this train will not move. And I'll tell you something else: while it's down the train won't stir no matter who you are – even if you're the stationmaster's son'!

There are pleasant little cottages on the right as we leave the station. After them, on the same side, we notice a circular copse. This is Ballykisteen House. A dramatic feature looms on the left horizon. The very pointed hill farthest ahead is Duntryleague. Stretching back are Moorabbey Hill, Slievenamuck and Bansha Wood near Tipperary town.

The novelty of the constabulary reorganised by Sir Robert Peel (1788-1850) and nicknamed 'Peelers' inspired Bansha's Darby Ryan to write the immortal ballad 'The Peeler and the Goat'.

> As Bansha peelers were, one night, on duty a patrolling O,
> They met a goat up on the road who seemed to be a strolling O,
> With bayonets fixed they sallied forth and caught her by the wizen O,
> And then swore out a mighty oath they'd send her off to prison O.

If we are keen of eye we may spot traces of Emly station, now derelict. The town on the right was called 'Imlagh' by the Greek astronomer and geographer Ptolmey, who named it one of the three principal cities of Ireland. Saint Ailbe founded an important church here in the sixth century. He was described as 'the other Patrick of Ireland' and as 'an Englishman by birth and an angel in conduct'.

He travelled extensively and would have welcomed the railroad to the spot that still bears his anglicised name. The saint's feast-day is on 12 September; special spiritual exercises were carried out on that date at St Ailbe's Well in Emly.

The see of Emly was united with Cashel's archbishopric by a 1568 act of parliament, and Emly was the cathedral town until 1718. The rapacious Miler Magrath was made archbishop in 1570. His favour with Queen Elizabeth allowed him to annex Lismore and Waterford, which he later forfeited for Killala and Achonry. He also held Down and Connor, but his juggling act serving Queen and Pope as he imprisoned friars for preaching against the throne, lost him the northern see. He lived to be a hundred.

We will be mentioning Emly again later, in connection with a War of Independence incident, but let us leave it in a lighter vein as we recall the wealthy passenger on the Cork-bound train who availed of a short stop at the station to step out on the platform and deeply breathe in the fresh air of Tipperary. He struck his expanded chest with his fist and remarked to a porter 'Isn't this invigorating!'

'No sir,' replied the porter, 'It's in Tipperary.'

CHAPTER FIVE

CO. LIMERICK and CO. CORK

Mention County Limerick and an Irishman thinks of its western portion with Shannon airport and estuary, its historical Danish city of the Treaty Stone, Foynes and the modern Shannon town. Our journey hops briefly into an eastern corner, where the county steals a good third of the Golden Vale and some of the Galtee range from Tipperary.

A seventeenth-century writer, Thomas Dineley, described Limerick women as '...favoured and fair handed, big, large, well-bottomed, not laced but suffered to grow at will...'[12] He made *no bones* about what songwriters have known before and since – that Limerick has beautiful ladies!

We know we are approaching Knocklong, just inside the Limerick border, when we see the remains of a castle clinging to a small bare hillside on the left. It is all that remains of a sixteenth century O'Hurley keep. Lucky passengers might see the celebrated Scarteen hunt pass the cairn alongside, for this is the county over which it chases the fox. And an establishment visible from Knocklong station called 'The Horseshoe Hotel' reminds us of the tradition.

The Ryan family hunted with the pack for 200 years and Thady Ryan was its master for a record forty-one years from 1946 to 1987. After that, he moved to Canterbury, New Zealand, to foster a new development in mating between the blood lines of Irish draught and New Zealand thoroughbred horses. The Scarteen Hunt is nicknamed 'The Black and Tans' — apt, for the railway station which we are entering figured in Ireland's struggle for independence. Indeed, the incident was one which brought about the imposition of the dreaded 'Tans' on that campaign. And again, Limerick robbed glory from its neighbour, because it was Tipperarymen who effected the celebrated 'Knocklong Rescue'.

Said Lloyd George to Macpherson, 'I'll give you the sack.
For to govern Ireland you have not the knack.
I'll send over Greenwood, a much stronger man
And he'll do my work with the bold Black and Tan'.

An attack against two policemen escorting gelignite at Soloheadbeg, Tipperary on 21 January 1919 marked the beginning of the War of Independence. Dan Breen, Seamus Robinson, Seán Treacy and a young man named Seán Hogan were prominent in that action. Martial law was enforced in the area and Hogan was captured. The IRA heard that he was to be moved under heavy guard by train to Cork for his trial, so they decided to rescue him at Knocklong. Four volunteers boarded the train at Emly while Breen, Treacy, Robinson and Ned O'Brien cycled across the Limerick border and waited at Knocklong. A signal was given from the train that Hogan was on board.

Seán Treacy leaped aboard and discovered Hogan sitting handcuffed between two RIC constables. Two armed militia men sat opposite. O'Brien moved up alongside and both rescuers drew revolvers. The policemen tried to shield themselves with their prisoner as they opened fire. One of them was shot dead before the other threw himself out the window of the train and fled.

Treacy struggled with a police sergeant and got shot in the throat. He managed to fire on the sergeant, killing him. Dan Breen came upon another constable who was just about to open fire on his colleague. Both men fired and although Breen was shot in the lungs, he disarmed his assailant.

Seán Hogan was seized and all escaped — Breen, be it said, with the assistance of a British army private named Fox, who was of Irish birth. This soldier was later court-martialled and imprisoned, after a death sentence was commuted. Two local volunteers, Pat Maher and Ned Foley, were executed at Mountjoy in June 1921 for the Knocklong affair. Medical opinion gave Breen no hope of surviving his wound, but he continued with the struggle for independence and opposed the pro-Treaty forces afterwards, in the Civil War. Disgusted at its outcome, he went to the United States where he ran a speak-easy during the Prohibition period. He later served as a Dáil deputy and attempted to establish a film industry here. Dan Breen died in 1969.

Soon after leaving Knocklong we see the Gothic spire of SS Peter and Paul's church at Kilmallock ahead. Apt, because the name means the 'Church of Mo Cheallog', a seventh century saint. An early Fitzgerald stronghold, the town suffered considerably during the Desmond wars. One lord and his countess were surprised by an English raid during a severe winter; they were forced to spend a night immersed to the chin in the River Loobagh, to avoid capture. In the town's church too, James Fitzmaurice, the 'Súgán' Earl of Desmond, submitted to Elizabeth I after an ignominious capitulation. What happened was this:

Perrot, the Lord President of Munster — possibly weary of the carnage that resulted from mighty battles — challenged James Fitzmaurice, the Captain of Desmond, to single combat at Kilmore Wood. Perrot envisaged a grand *affaire d'honneur* decided by sword, lance and shield. The challenge was brought to Fitzmaurice by a convict on parole and he accepted on condition that he would name the terms himself.

He wanted the joust to be fought on Irish cobs, an immediate disadvantage to Perrot who was banking on a tall mount to make best use of the long lance against his heavier opponent. But gallantly, he accepted. Then Fitzmaurice sent a message that he despised the British battledress and suggested that they wear Irish costumes, dispense with lances and fight with broad Irish sword and dagger. Against all advice, Perrot again agreed.

A light rain was falling at the appointed hour of the selected day. Perrot arrived, regaled in a copious saffron cape above wide scarlet breeches. He waited — and waited. His disapproving captains glared up at him from the valley, appalled at his being kept waiting by a mere Irish earl. Still there was no sign of Fitzmaurice and just as a furious Perrot was about to depart, a messenger arrived with a parchment from his foe. It read, 'If I do kill the great Sir John Perrot, the Queen of England will but send another President into this province; but if he do kill me, there is none in Ireland to succeed me or command as I now do'.

Perrot became a subject of ridicule at Whitehall, whose officials were enraged that an English governor was made a stooge by a roguish Irishman. Dressed like a court jester and becoming drenched in an Irish mist on a Munster hill — the very thought of it! The Irish laughed, but the British government gained its revenge by introducing a blockade that set out to starve the Irish forces into submission.

The ploy worked. Early in 1573, the 'Súgán' Earl came to Kilmallock and knelt in submission to Perrot who held a sword to his adversary's breast as he accepted surrender.

Later, Oliver Cromwell used the King's Castle at Kilmallock as a field hospital and ordnance depot and the town has a thirteenth-century Dominican abbey which was restored in the fourteenth and fifteenth centuries.

The town's history is not all belligerent however. The eighteenth-century Gaelic poet, Andrias MacCraith is buried beside the Church of SS Peter and Paul. He was known as *An Mangaire Sugach* — 'The Merry Pedlar' (or more often, 'The Tipsy Hawker'), and was a sort of Irish Robbie Burns. He wandered about composing verse and singing songs for a few drinks. Short of money for imbibing once, he became a Protestant for a few weeks; but a minister evicted him from his congregation for his waywardness. His own Church refused to have him back, so he satirised its clergy. The incident inspired some of his most tragic and worthwhile poems.

'Is fánach faon mé, is fraoch mhar fuar é,' began one. Translated, its first verse went:

Kilmallock Abbey, Co. Limerick

> A wanderer and spiritless am I
> Wretched on the mountain top
> With none, alas, to befriend me
> Except heather and the north wind.

In his old age he still walked Munster's roads. He died poverty-stricken in the tumbledown shed of a stranger.

Out of Kilmallock there is a thick wooded area over on the left. This is Mount Coote, birthplace of Sir Eyre Coote who conquered Hyder Ali (1722-1782), the Muhammadan soldier/adventurer and leader who was the most formidable Asiatic rival the British ever encountered in India.

Just after this we pass the spot that is the butt of more Irish jokes than the shillelagh itself. A party of Irish volunteers were being briefed about demolishing a bridge in the place.

'I want you to go out tonight and blow up the Effin bridge,' instructed their leader.

'What effin' bridge?' asked a volunteer.

A ridge appears on the left-hand horizon. This is Ballyhowra mountain range. Half of it is in Co. Limerick, half in Co. Cork. As we enter the 'Rebel County' we recall its great hurling tradition, so cherished that a new bridge opened in 1987 in its chief city is called after Christy Ring. And the pride of its people is certified by a plaque on that same bridge which tells that no great national figure was called in to perform the opening ceremony. Their own Lord Mayor was considered a worthy enough personage.

The county's part in the nation's struggle is legendary; its disposition towards preserving its culture and traditions is not lauded but becomes apparent even to the casual visitor.

Over on the right a town appears and a towering dairy plant indicates that it is Rath Luirc or Charleville.

> You asked me for to sing a song
> And to please you I will try,
> I'll sing to you about a town
> That is known to you and I.
> Although three thousand miles away,
> My heart it lies there still,
> It's the place my eyes first saw the light,
> It's the town of Charleville.
>
> — Thomas Reidy (1873-1915)[13]

Mail-trains did not stop at Charleville and it was therefore one of the many stations that boasted a 'snatcher'. Near the Effin road bridge was placed a small Post Office hut on the front of which a net was slung. A Charleville postman brought the mail by bicycle and on 'Shank's mare' to this spot and deposited the mail in a stout leather bag. He hung this on an arm and it was 'snatched' by the speeding train on its way to Dublin. In an instantaneous operation, the train dropped its post into the net and the postman brought this back to Charleville.

The countryside here is flat and we wonder why the railway line was not laid closer to the comparatively modern town. Well, it seems that a big landowner, Colonel Harrison, would not allow the line to cut through his estate (on our right) and so the directors had to settle for a station about three kilometres away.

Castle Harrison was the local 'Big House' and it is interesting to note that, in 1846, 'Indian Meal Flour' was distributed and 1s. 6^1/$_2$d. per stone deducted from tenants' accounts. They had to give up to three days labour to clear this debt.

Charleville was named after Charles II, by the Earl of Orrery, Lord President of Munster. It was called Rathcogan between 1290 and 1671 (and later as Rathgogan or Rathgoggan) after a descendant of the Cambro-Norman adventurer, Miles de Cogan.

The poet Seán Clarach MacDomhnaill (1691-1754) is buried in Charleville. His farm became the seat of the Courts of Poetry, over which he presided, in the eighteenth century. People like Eoghan Roe Ó Suilleabhain, Seán Ó Tuama and Liam Dall Ó h-Iffernán attended.

A tyrant landlord called Colonel Dawson refused twigs that fell from his trees to the poor and drew down Seán's wrath. After the tyrant's death, c.1738, Seán wrote a merciless satire which included the line 'Squeeze down his bones, o ye stones'. It antagonised so much that he was forced to take refuge abroad.

After the death of his father at a village near Mallow, Thomas W. Croke, the future archbishop, lived here with his uncle, a parish priest. He was educated at the classical endowed school. Later, in 1849, he replaced his brother, Fr William Croke, who died of famine fever in the town; he served in that capacity until 1853.[14] Another celebrated

Charleville cleric was An tAthar Peadar Ó Laoghaire. In his *Mo Scéal Féin*, he devotes chapters to his life as curate in 'An Rath', yet another old Irish name for the town. Secondary education was provided here for Eamon de Valera. He walked the seven miles from Bruree ('Residence of Kings') in Limerick. A branch railway to Bruree existed since 1861 but the guardians of the young student who was to make history could not afford the fare. That branch line was later extended to Patrickswell, Croom and Rosstemple. One day a porter at the station after Bruree called 'Patrickswell, Patrickswell', and a youthful passenger answered 'So is Mick and so am I'.

Charleville also housed the well-known musical brothers, the Sylvesters, during a number of winters. Chris and Ralph had bands on the Irish circuit; Victor became an acknowledged exponent of 'strict tempo' ballroom music through his popular BBC programme.

A small headstone erected to a Denis Cavanagh stands in Charleville cemetery. Its inscription is in crude and irregular calligraphy. It says:

> Denis Cavanagh, died 1st February '92. Aged 1002.

Let's move on from here before we become older than Methuselah!

> Once I strayed from Charleville
> As careless as could be;
> I wandered over plain and hill
> Until I reached the sea.

The above rhyme was attributed to James Clarence Mangan (1803-1849) but we do not have time to probe the validity of the claim because there is so much still to recall before our journey's end.

After a long period heading in a south-west direction, the track finally rights itself to a south-bound course. Across the Awbeg river, Castle Harrison, of which we made mention, stands on the right. It may be lost, because the train is picking up speed on a three kilometre straight. A pleasant village called Newtown is passed before we spot a road sign announcing the main Charleville-Buttevant road which continues on a course parallel with ours for a kilometre or so. The track curves to its contour, the train reduces speed and we are entering Buttevant. The town was founded by the Anglo-Norman de Barrys after land seizure from the McCarthys in the twelfth and thirteenth centuries. Some sources claim that the name is a derivative of *Boutez-en-avant* (Press Forward), the war-cry of the de Barrys. More widely accepted is the view that it was given the Norman-French name for a defensive outwork — *botavant*. Cill na Mallach, its Irish name, is reflected in Edmund Spenser's 'Colin Clouts Come Home Again':

> Mulla, the daughter of old Mole so hight
> The nymph which of that water course hath charge,
> That springing out of Mole, doth run down right
> To Buttevant, where spreading forth at large
> It giveth name unto that cittie
> Which Kilnemullah cleped is of old.

Along this route marched the 'Wild Geese' who took their name from the wild fowl of the woods of Annagh nearby. And a strange story seeks an explanation in their stop at Walshestown which touches on Buttevant parish.

A humble cottier named Lombard dreamed three nights in succession that if he travelled to Limerick and stood on its main bridge he would find his fortune. The poor man walked the journey and did as he was bid but there was no sign of any reward. Then a cobbler who had observed him approached and asked why he was standing around so long. Lombard admitted his foolishness and was sympathised with by the shoemaker who said he too was afflicted by a recurring dream. It told him that under a whitethorn bush in the garden of a man named Lombard from Buttevant, there was a crock of gold.

Lombard rushed home and dug under the whitethorn in his garden. He found gold lying on a large flagstone. There was an inscription on the stone which gave a decorative effect so he placed it at the back of his hearth. Years later, an itinerant teacher informed him that the calligraphy was in Latin and that it meant 'Under This Lies More'. Lombard said nothing but went out during the night, dug further and accumulated vast wealth in gold — so much that he built Lombard Castle at the south end of the town.

That tale is strange but even more peculiar is a report that in March 1905 a man from Walshestown named William Twomey was working with a Robert Mahoney repairing a wall. As they worked, William told how he had a dream in which a lady told him to place his hands in his pockets and when he did he discovered gold and silver coins. As he finished his story the couple prised a stone from the wall and to their amazement, sixteen silver coins and two gold ones tumbled out. Some were from the reign of Charles II, dated 1677 and 1679 and others were Spanish of the same period. It is thought that a soldier of the 'Wild Geese' may have robbed a comrade and hidden the loot for later collection.

The Awbeg river flows through Buttevant and neighbouring ancient Doneraile, where one of Ireland's 'immortal trees', a 300-year-old ash, grows. Spenser lived at Kilcolman Castle. As well as the poem quoted above he wrote the acclaimed *Fairie Queene, View of the Present State of Ireland*, the *Amoretti Sonnets* and *Epithalamium*. At Doneraile Court, Mary, wife of the first Viscount Doneraile hid herself in a grandfather clock to find out what went on at a Freemason lodge meeting. She was discovered and made to take the initiation oath so that she would not reveal what she had heard. Thus she became the first female mason.

In 1781, Lord Doneraile closed all Mass houses on his estate when an eighty-year-old parish priest excommunicated a man living in adultery. The cleric refused to lift the excommunication, so Doneraile had his housekeeper and himself horsewhipped. Tried for, and found guilty of, common assault, damages of £1,000 were awarded against Doneraile. This was so unexpected that Thomas Davis referred to it as 'the first spoils of emancipation'.[15]

Spenser's progeny sold Doneraile to the Lord President of Munster, Warham St Leger — and that is why we have strayed a few kilometres off the track, so to speak. It was to the spire of St Leger Church that the first point-to-point steeplechase took place, starting from Buttevant. That was in 1752. And still with equestrian topics, Napoleon's horse Morengo (formerly Hidalgo) was purchased at Buttevant fair.

In the early days of rail, a bishop arrived at Buttevant sitting alone in a third-class compartment. He had a ruddy complexion and was somewhat short-tempered. He almost resented the intrusion of a common labourer who entered and sat opposite. He became even more annoyed when the intruder addressed him, saying, 'Are you a curate, your reverence?' The bishop answered frigidly, 'No, but I used to be,' whereupon the labourer adopted a sympathetic tone and said, 'Ah dear, it's terrible what drink does to a man'.

A disaster occurred here on 1 August 1980, killing eighteen passengers and injuring seventy-five.

Still heading directly south, we arrive into more typical Irish landscape. Green modulations carry the interested eye along towards rich purples and earthy browns in the Boggeragh (right) and Nagles (left) ahead.

A railway yard on the left is full of assorted rolling stock of various vintages. One carriage has a legend emblazoned on its side: 'The Great Southern Railway Preservation Society, Mallow'. Container cargo is piled on the right. This is sugar-beet and dairy produce country and Mallow station bears witness to a vigorous local economy.

In ancient O'Keeffe territory, Magh Ella (Plain of Ella) was an important ford on the Blackwater and a castle still remains to remind us of this.

Roches and Geraldines of Desmond were prominent in

Mallow Castle, Co. Cork

establishing the town before it was handed over to the Lord President of Munster, Sir Thomas Norreys. But the English fled Mallow, after burning it. That was after Hugh O'Neill's Yellow Ford victory and the subsequent rising in

Munster. Jephsons acquired the town through a convenient marriage, and Cromwell captured its castle in 1643. Later, the place became a fashionable spa and was called 'The Bath of Ireland'. Munster swains who did not appreciate the distinction considered this an insult; they retorted with, 'Many a dirty blackguard from across the water washed in it, right enough'.

But while they protested they joined in the fun of the resort, indulged in by a lively, energetic Anglo-Irish set whose wild behaviour inspired the traditional Irish air called 'The Rakes of Mallow'. All sorts of lyrics have accompanied it down the years, including:

> Mickey Mackey had a hen
> Who laid eggs for gentlemen;
> Sometimes nine and sometimes ten —
> Poached for the Rakes of Mallow.

Mr and Mrs Samuel Carter Hall who in 1841 published their impressions of their tour of Ireland, called Mallow 'a pretty and agreeable town...much frequented by invalid visitors'. Whiskey mixed with the spa waters that gushed from the 'Dogs' Heads' was a potent and stimulating drink, it was said. But curative claims on behalf of the waters are dismissed by modern scientists. With the assistance of a European grant, Cork County Council bored to eighty metres and found water of 19.7° Celsius (almost 68° Fahrenheit) with the intention of heating Mallow swimming pool and its County Hospital. The hot springs are brought about by heat sources below, fissures which allow the warmth to rise, equilibrium of water supplies and a cap rock to insulate. These features remove the mystique from the phenomenon which began in 1728 when a Mrs Wellstead claimed a miraculous cure. Subterranean happenings also occurred in 1868 when there was an earthquake in the area. It was noted by An t-Athar Peadar Ó Laoghaire in *Mo Scéal Féin*.

Anthony Trollope and Elizabeth Bowen lived for a while in Mallow. Thomas Davis, poet and founder of *The Nation* newspaper was born here in 1814. William O'Brien, editor of the Land League journal *United Ireland* was also Mallow-born (1852). He was later an MP for the town. It was he who, in 1910, led some Cork members of parliament in the 'All for Ireland League'. Their motto was 'Conference, Conciliation, Consent'. Eighty years later the call could still be invoked!

There is another beloved son – Patrick Augustine (Canon) Sheehan, whose *My New Curate, Glenanaar* and *The Graves at Kilmorna* were essential reading for scholars of the early century.

During the War of Independence, Liam Lynch, supported by Ernie O'Malley, raided Mallow barracks. Described as the only IRA capture of an occupied military barracks, it was a daring operation:

> The post was occupied by the 17th Lancers, whose crest was a death's head and who were dubbed 'The Death or Glories'. The newly-formed flying column of Lynch's brigade brought off the coup. Acting as scouts in a complicated manoeuvre were the local Mallow company who steered the raiders through the constant patrols of military and Black and Tans.
>
> Two of the barrack maintenance staff, Jack Bolster and Dick Willis, reported on the movements of guards, sentries and look-outs within the gates. They provided sketches and answered questions put to them by Lynch, Paddy O'Brien, George Power and Ernie O'Malley. Willis brought Lynch and O'Malley on a tour of the barrack surrounds and the area where the Lancer officers exercised their horses each morning.
>
> On the morning of the raid the local RIC barracks was covered by Volunteers. Paddy McCarthy of Newmarket, posing as a Board of Works overseer, entered with Willis and Bolster.
>
> When the officers cantered out on their horses they left an NCO, Sergeant Gibbs, in charge of the post. Ernie O'Malley approached the gate and presented a bogus

letter for personal delivery to a member of the garrison. He was refused admission but he overpowered the gatekeeper sentry and waved on the remainder of the attacking party to take over the guardroom. Gibbs rushed to train a machine-gun on the now wide open main gate. One burst of fire could have wiped out the attackers so he was shot, and he fell. After IRA Volunteers had cut all communications into Mallow, motor cars were driven into the barracks and loaded with captured weapons and ammunition even as the last of the garrison were being disarmed and held. Field dressings were applied to Gibbs' wound but he was past medical help. Up to thirty assorted arms and some bayonets were captured.

Members of the column spread straw and petrol with the intention of firing the barracks but the urgent shrill blast of the retreat whistle signal prevented this operation being completed. Men jumped into cars, well satisfied with their success. As they passed along the road, willing hands sawed down trees in their wake. Mesmerised officers dismounted from their chargers. Awe changed to anger and an enraged garrison began a campaign of arson and general destruction of property in the town and its hinterland.[16]

During the civil war the fine ten-arched viaduct by which we cross over the Blackwater was destroyed. An early road-bridge at Mallow was swept away by a great flood on 28 September 1628. As we cross the river we get a panoramic view of the town left behind while we sidle close to the main Cork road.

In the river valley below the mountains ahead, about four miles to our left, is Killavullen (or Ballymoy). From near that spot a young man emigrated to France and became an officer in Dillon's regiment, fighting at Dottingen and Fontenoy. After retirement and marriage to a cousin he settled in Cognac and established a distillery which still produces brandy that bears his name — Hennessy. Small wonder we wandered off course to document the fact! Let it be said also, however, that Nano

Nagle (1728-1784), foundress of the Presentation order of nuns, hailed from the same area.

As we slide into the valley of the River Clyda, we see traces of a station called after Mourne Abbey. This was a preceptory of the Knights Hospitallers of St John of Jerusalem, possibly founded by Alexander de Sancta Helena before 1216. A bloody battle took place there in 1520, between the forces of the Earl of Desmond and Cormac Óg McCarthy of Muskerry. A thousand men died.

Again we see the main road alongside, and a prominent sign to Burnfoot. The name stems from a ring fort and close by there have been finds of an ogham stone, a cremation pit and other items of archaeological interest. Past what is left of Rathduff station we speed along the valley of the River Martin.

An enterprising clergyman, Canon Matt Horgan (1776-1849) from Waterloo, close to the railway and near Blarney, decided that the townland needed some antiquities so he set about building crannogs, a round tower and all the paraphernalia of an ancient settlement. Some of their remains can still be seen today.

Before a distinct curve to the left, we may catch a glimpse of the renowned Blarney Castle on the right.

> The Blarney train came down Fair Lane
> Like a devil from holy water...

Henry Ford called his Michigan home 'Fair Lane' after the Cork street where his grandfather lived (now Wolfe Tone St). The verse refers to the Cork and Muskerry Light Railway, affectionately known as 'The Blarney Tram'. It had bamboo carriages with openings that didn't have glass — lovely on a fine day but howling wind-traps during inclement weather. It wound its tree-covered way and had a recognised stop at Moxley's Inn. Passengers refreshed themselves and completed their journey in high spirits till they reached the terminus close by the castle with the most famous stone in the world.

Blarney Castle, Co. Cork

There's a Blarney stone in Dublin,
There's a Blarney stone in Clare
There's a Blarney stone in Wicklow
And another in Kildare...

If you believe the song, don't tell it to a Corkman, for no rock — not even the one upon which Peter built his Church – was ever extolled in lyrics like the one that has given a new word to the English language. It has been kissed by people of all ages and from all over the globe in the hope that they would have the Irish 'gift of the gab' bestowed upon them.

> If the Blarney stone stood out in Sydney Harbour
> And County Cork at Adelaide did appear
> Erin's sons would never roam...

The tradition of kissing the stone may have arisen because the MacCarthys of Muskerry kept a bardic school there — and nobody can *plámás* like a poet! Or perhaps the tale is true about the chieftain, Cormac MacDermot MacCarthy's repeated promises to renounce the traditional system of electing chieftains and take tenure of his lands from the Crown instead. Deputy Carew kept reminding him to 'come in off his keeping', but 'with fair words and soft speech' MacCarthy postponed, again and again, the formalities associated with the agreement. An impatient Queen Elizabeth was told once more that MacCarthy said he was about to surrender his rights, whereupon she announced, 'This is all Blarney, what he says, he never means'. Thus was initiated the word that suggests pleasant talk intended to deceive without causing offence.

The Irish writer, Bryan MacMahon, told how he and his wife were interviewed in the United States for a St Patrick's Day programme. Asked if they had ever kissed the Blarney stone, Bryan said he had but Mrs MacMahon shook her head. The banner newspaper headline over the interview on 17 March read:

> MacMAHON STATES THAT HE HAS OFTEN KISSED THE BLARNEY STONE, BUT NOT HIS WIFE.[17]

CHAPTER SIX

DESTINATION

A severe camber tilts the train to the left, but on the right, above a ridge, traces of Cork city appear, aerial masts and other paraphernalia of commerce. Through a deep ravine then and a seven-arched bridge in a glen below on the left distracts. Not for long, however.

The grey bulk of Collins Barracks appears, reminding us that we left a similarly named bastion at Dublin. Beckoning later, St Mary's Cathedral (better known in Cork as the North Chapel), St Finbarr's fine triple-spired cathedral and in between, in a light raw-drisheen red, is Shandon.

St Finbarr's Cathedral, Cork City

> The night the goat broke loose upon the Parade
> All the shawlies on the Coal Quay were afraid
> A hundred thousand people
> Tried to climb up Shandon steeple
> The night the goat broke loose upon the Parade.

Cut-stone walls near the railway line bear graffiti of a city which had one Lord Mayor who died on hunger-strike and another who was murdered, and which had its centre gutted by fire — all part of a nation's birth pangs:

> We aim to be free
> A story about Cork and freedom.

Just a brief, tempting glance of the city is offered and then we are in a long tunnel — the better to meditate on the wonders that are in stone, as all of Cork's grand old town is at our feet. We can be sporting and playing in the green leafy shade from here on!

In the early days of rail, an excited young boy noticed the train swaying and rocking as it approached this tunnel. He shouted, 'Oh jaysus, the train is going to miss the hole'. And an old woman from Buttevant was going to visit an oculist and thought she was going blind when the old steam engine thundered into it. She bred yet another Irish bull as she screamed, 'I'm blint, I'm blint; I can see nothing but a woeful noise'.

There is no such unpleasant din at Kent station, named after a young patriot, Thomas Kent who, along with his brothers was surrounded by armed members of the Royal Irish Constabulary at his Castlelyons home after the Easter Week 1916 Rising. His brother, Richard, died from wounds received in the ensuing gunbattle. Thomas was later arrested and was executed on 9 May 1916.

A bronze plaque outside the terminus commemorates him but inside, pride of place is seized by the shining Steam-Engine No. 36, a locomotive built in 1848 for the GS & W Railway. It hauled mainline trains until withdrawn from service in 1874, having completed 487,918 miles. Its

The steam-engine 'Slieve Gullion'

twenty-three tons of engineering nostalgia is a statement of pride — just like the 'Cork 800' display opposite it which gives a resumé of some of the main events in Cork's colourful history, viz:

030	Death of St Finbarr
822,833,839,1013	Cork attacked by Vikings
1229	Dominican Abbey Founded
1541	Crown Plunders Monasteries
1603	Rebellion against James I
1633	City Damaged by Floods
1688	Arrival of James II
1690	Siege by Williamite Forces
1750	Bells of Shandon installed
1838	Fr Matthew Launches his Total Abstinence Crusade
1838	First East to West Atlantic Steamship Crossing by SS *Sirius*, Cork to New York

1859	St Patrick's Bridge Built
1902-1903	Great Exhibition Visited by Edward VII
1920	Tomás McCurtain Murdered. Terence Mac Swiney Dies on Hunger-Strike
1955	Cork Opera House Destroyed by Fire
1963	Visit of John F. Kennedy, President of the USA
1965	New Opera House Opened

Shandon Steeple, Cork City

An international Apprentice Competition in 1975 and the construction of City Centre Park in 1985 complete the list — but then the display was designed and executed by the Painting and Decorating Department of AnCO, Cork!

View from Patrick's Hill, Cork City

Leave Kent station and note the busy Cork-Dublin road. High above, Montenotte's turned-up nose; her window eyes staring ahead, avoiding a downcast peep that might discover a weary traveller. Walk a little towards the city centre and glance back at the railway station. Gently and elegantly curved, the black and white platform contrasts with the red brick to give a model train complex appearance. A setting sun picks out cranes and ships' funnels in the background. Turn your back if you can on this physical appeal. On a sign opposite read:

POPULATION 136,000

Twinned with COVENTRY and RENNES
VILLE JUMELÉE AVEC CORK & RENNES

And above all this international cameraderie:

CORK CITY — FÁILTE

REFERENCES

1. Lewis, Samuel, *A History and Topography of Dublin City and County*, Reprinted Dublin & Cork 1980.

2. Costello, Con, 'Looking Back' 193. Grand Canal Advertisement, *Leinster Leader*.

3. Costello, Con 'Looking Back' 46, *Leinster Leader*.

4. O'Connor, Pat, Pamphlet, NLI P2070.

5. Egan, Desmond, *Collected Poems*, USA / Newbridge 1984.

6. O'Farrell, Padraic, *Life Train–Thoughtful and Trivial*, Dublin 1982.

7. Kitchen, Paddy, *Gerald Manley Hopkins*, London 1978.

8. Crossley, F.W., *Tales of the Rail*, Dublin 1904.

9. An Irish Priest, *An Irish Priest in Maryboro and Mountjoy*, Dublin 1919, NLI IR 9410.

10. Mulligan, Fergus, *One Hundred and Fifty Years of Irish Railways*, Belfast 1983.

11. Limerick Town Council Railway Committee Report, NLI P2070.

12. 'Extracts from the Journal of Thomas Dineley', RSAIJ IV (1856-57).

13. Meaghar, Jim & O'Riordan, Ted, *Charleville and District Historical Journal*, Charleville 1986.

14. Ibid.

15. Corish, Patrick J., *The Catholic Community in the 17th and 18th Centuries*, Dublin 1981.

16. O'Farrell, Padraic, *The Ernie O'Malley Story*, Dublin & Cork 1983.

17. MacMahon, Bryan, *Here's Ireland*, Dublin 1982.

ANOTHER INTERESTING TITLE

IN THE TRACKS OF THE WEST CLARE RAILWAY
Edmund Lenihan

Far more people have heard of the West Clare Railway than ever travelled on it. Far more talk about it than have ever seen any part of it. For this Percy French's famous song 'Are Ye Right There, Michael?' is responsible. *In The Tracks Of The West Clare Railway* is at once a history of this, the last of the Irish narrow-gauge lines, a tourist's guide to a relatively little known part of Clare, a record of a walking journey along what remains of the line from Ennis to Kilkee/Kilrush, and a tribute to the people and county of Clare.

Anyone with even a superficial acquaintance with Clare will know what a wealth of varied scenery it contains, together with abundant archaeological sites and historical remains spanning 5000 years and more of human habitation. Not the least of these are the earthworks of the West and South Clare Railways. Eddie Lenihan believes that a time will come when parts of these lines will be preserved as national monuments, but until that happens their gradual destruction will go on apace. For what was a railway is now a disjointed succession of pieces linking not just places, but in a way two worlds, one unhurried and traditional, the other brash, frenzied and modern.

But though trains are unlikely ever again to run between Ennis and Kilkee the legend of this little branch line of the southern railway system will live on as long as there are people who look back fondly on the past.